New Edition plus

Viewfinder

Topics

Ethnic Diversity in the UK

An Imagined Community?

compiled and edited
by
Michael Mitchell

Langenscheidt

Berlin · München · Wien · Zürich · New York

Viewfinder

Topics – New Edition plus

Unterrichtsmaterialien für die Sekundarstufe II

Ethnic Diversity in the UK

An Imagined Community?

Herausgeber:
Prof. em. Dr. Dr. h.c. mult. Peter Freese

Autor:
Dr. Michael Mitchell

Projekt-Team:
Dr. Martin Arndt, Münster
Prof. Dr. Mita Banerjee, Siegen
David Beal, M. A., Bochum
Cornelia Becker, Bremen
Dr. Peter Dines, Cert. Ed., Ludwigsburg
Prof. i. R. Dr. Hanspeter Dörfel, Ludwigsburg
Prof. Dr. Sabine Doff, Frankfurt/Main
Dr. Claudia Drawe, Essen
OStR Dieter Düwel, Castrop-Rauxel
Prof. em. Dr. Dr. h.c. Dr. h. c. Peter Freese, Paderborn
Dr. Carin Freywald †
Dr. Christine Gottstein-Strobl, Eichstätt
Jennifer von der Grün, B. A., Dortmund
OStR Ulrich Imig, Wildeshausen
OStR Reimer Jansen, Oyten-Sagehorn
Dr. Michael Mitchell, M. A., Reken und Warwick
Prof. Dr. Michael Porsche, Paderborn
StD i. E. Detlef Rediker, Lippstadt
StD Dr. Peter-J. Rekowski, Kirchhain
StD i.K. Peter Ringeisen, M. A., Amberg
Karl Sassenberg, Münster
StD Henning Scholz †
StD Dr. Annegret Schrick, Essen
OStR Ekkehard Sprenger, Kiel
StR Susanne Stadler, Wiesbaden
OStD Dr. Dietrich Theißen †
Donald Turner, M. A. †
Prof. Dr. Laurenz Volkmann, Jena
Philip Wade, M. A., Cert. Ed., Amberg

Verlagsredaktion: Dr. Beatrix Finke
Visuelles Konzept: Barbara Slowik, Atelier S., München
Layout und Produktion: kaltnermedia GmbH, Bobingen
www.langenscheidt.de/viewfinder

Umwelthinweis: Gedruckt auf chlorfrei gebleichtem Papier.

1. Auflage 2010

Printed in Germany
ISBN 978-3-526-51032-1

10010

Contents

* Titles provided by the editor

Ethnic Diversity in the UK

At Uphall primary school in Ilford, East London, pupils speak 52 different home languages. The 28 children in the picture speak 23 different languages. "It's like a micro world," says head teacher Andrew Morrish. "We have got children from all corners of the globe." One in three of the children at the school come from a Pakistani background, but the cultures represented also include eastern European, Chinese, Afro-Caribbean, Russian and African. Despite these varied ethnic backgrounds, the school has recently been praised by the school inspectors: "The inspectors judge this to be an outstanding school ... Standards are rising and pupils achieve well, in spite of the fact that almost all have English as an additional language." (reported in *The Independent*, 26 July 2006)

Ashim Rehman, 11, has attended Uphall primary school for seven years. "I've got lots of friends there. We speak Urdu at home all the time, but I was born here and don't need any special help with English."

Irma Kliucininkaite, 11, was born in Lithuania and came to Britain aged three with her parents and baby brother. "When I first started at the school they took me into a class with other children who spoke all different languages and who couldn't speak English. Once I could speak a bit more I went back to the general class and got books that helped me learn English as well."

Eliana Jesus, 11, speaks Portuguese, French and English. She was born in Portugal to a Portuguese mother and an African father but the family came to Britain when she was a toddler. "My friends at school come from lots of different countries in Africa and India."

Pranav Patel, 10, speaks fluent Gujurati and English. His parents came from India but Pranav was born in the UK. "All the children in my class speak English but lots speak other languages at home. I speak Gujurati if I'm talking to my auntie or my grandma but when I talk to my sisters or my mum and dad I speak English. I'm from India – well, I was born here, I'm English – but I'm from India as well."

An Imagined Community?

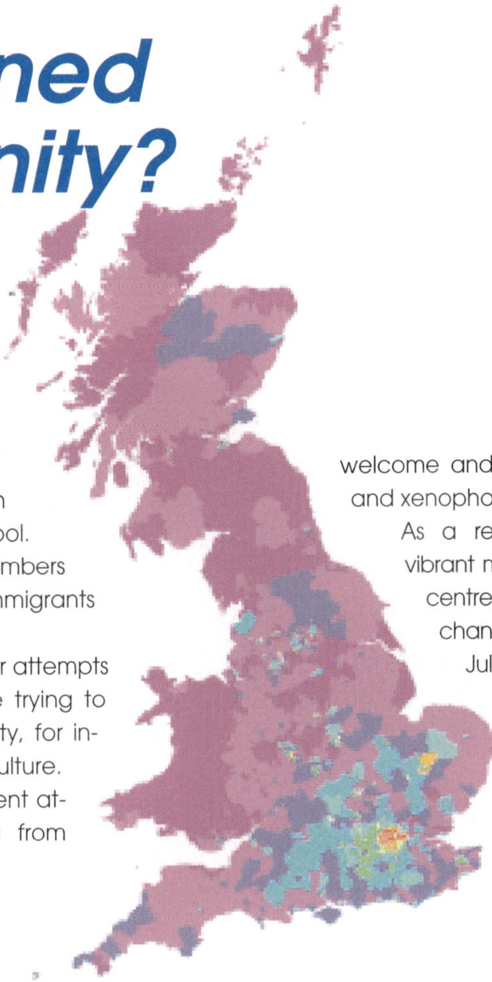

The United Kingdom is a country of increasing ethnic diversity, as can be seen from the example of this school. Since the Second World War large numbers of people have entered the UK as immigrants or to seek asylum.

They have faced challenges in their attempts to integrate into British society while trying to preserve aspects of their own identity, for instance their language, religion and culture.

They have also experienced different attitudes from British society ranging from welcome and support to prejudice, racism and xenophobia.

As a result the UK has become a vibrant mixture of cultures and a global centre of financial and cultural exchange, but a series of bombings in July 2005 carried out by British men of Pakistani and Caribbean origin highlighted unanswered questions about identity, about what it means to be 'British'.

I want my children to go to a school where at our summer fair today the International Food Stall will sell, at a modest guess, the cuisine of 20 different countries. London can and does hold within it a diversity which astounds even visiting Americans – that melting-pot nation of immigrants … And since our children will grow up in a global economy, it is better they get used to it now.

(*Janice Turner,* The Times, *9 July 2005*)

1

Trevor Phillips

"Segregation and Integration"*

Trevor Phillips (b. 1953) belongs to a family which originally immigrated from Guyana in the West Indies. A journalist, politician and author, he was Chairman of the Commission for Racial Equality at the time he made this speech, which proved controversial. Some people were surprised that he was attacking 'multiculturalism' because he said Britain might be 'sleepwalking to segregation'. – 'After 7/7: Sleepwalking to Segregation', extract from a speech given at the Manchester Council for Community Relations, 22 September 2005.

The wreckage of the number 30 bus in Tavistock Square, London, in which Antony Fatayi-Williams and 14 others were killed on 7 July 2005. The suicide attacks have become known as 7/7.

On July 6, the day we won the Olympics of 2012, Britain emerged as a beacon for diversity across the globe. There is no doubt that the IOC saw London as a place where anyone, whatever their background, could come and feel at home, could visit and know they would find a kindred spirit.

This is a tribute to the team that put together the bid, to our capital city, but most of all to our nation. And it provides part of an answer to that currently vexed question: what is Britishness?

I would put that question differently now, and ask instead: what makes us British?

July 6 and the days after showed that one thing that makes us special is our comfort with diversity.

Even in the desperate adversity of the days that followed the London atrocities, the fact of our multiethnicity and our ease with it stood out. Those who died came from myriad backgrounds. Likewise, those who rescued the survivors and reassured the city. It became clear that the people who planted, or wanted to plant, bombs, stood alone, without the comfort of any community that would support their actions.

Earlier this month, as we watched the tragedy of New Orleans unfold, many people, I think – and some said this to me – consoled themselves with the thought that such a thing could never happen here.

By such a thing I do not mean the hurricane itself. I mean the manifest neglect of a poor, largely African American district, and the criminal disregard of citizens who did not have the resources to get out of the way of Katrina. The fact is that these people were socially, economically, culturally and psychologically marooned outside the mainstream of American society.

It wasn't that nobody cared about them. What happened was worse. The fact is that nobody who mattered even remembered that they existed. In a society where whites and blacks choose to live entirely separate lives, the black poor become invisible to the decision-makers and the powerful, unless and until they get themselves some guns and start to terrorise their own neighbours.

We, here, watching, could not imagine British people behaving like this.

Really?

Maybe we too have become blind to anything that isn't on the TV news or tabloid newspapers. Perhaps it's time that the cameras returned to the slow massacre of young men and women that is taking place on our streets in London, Manchester, Birmingham and Nottingham, for example. Perhaps it's time that the newspapers showed us the gang warfare that goes on just yards away from our front doors or in children's playgrounds, in communities we pass through but do not see.

We cannot and must not be complacent. We should learn from America's failure to act until they were in too deep to get out of the state they are now in.

The disastrous floods caused by Hurricane Katrina in New Orleans affected blacks far more than whites

Until New Orleans held up the mirror to the USA, Americans, too, prided themselves on having found the holy grail of integration, with black millionaires, academics, business people and politicians alongside the sports and entertainment stars.

But in New Orleans the truth broke the surface. It showed us a society in which the average black child still attends a black majority school. A society in which the average white person returns home at the day's end to all-white suburbs, where they won't see a non-white face until they go back to the city the next day. A democracy in which black politicians, with a few notable exceptions, represent black districts, gerrymandered in order to provide the minimum of black representation. An economy in which black businessmen sell their wares largely to a black middle class. And an education system in which most black academics are teaching at all-black colleges or in urban institutions disproportionately packed with ethnic minority students.

This is a segregated society, in which the one truth that is self-evident is that people cannot and never will be equal. That is why, for all of us who care about racial equality and integration, America is not our dream, but our nightmare.

I think here we also have a different idea of what integration means. There I think the focus is purely on equal rights for different groups. Amongst America's hyphenated identities, the part of their identity that marks them out as different seems to have become as important, even more important, than the part that binds them together. Americans have all fetched up at the same restaurant; but every group has its own separate table, with its own menu, its own waiters and its own way of paying the bill.

I think we have a richer interpretation here that prizes both our individuality and our nation over and above our ethnicity. There are some old-fashioned types who think of integration as just another word for assimilation. But no-one seriously believes that we should all speak, look, dress, worship and act the same.

However, there has to be a balance struck between an 'anything goes' multiculturalism on the one hand, which leads to deeper division and inequality; and on the other, an intolerant, repressive uniformity. We need a kind of integration that binds us together without stifling us. We need to be a nation of many colours that combine to create a single rainbow. [...]

Too much that is too abstract is already being said on the subject of Britishness, but there are some simple truths that should bind us together.

First and foremost, our shared values: for example an attachment to democracy, freedom of speech, and equality, values which anyone who expects to live in Britain must respect and abide by, both notionally and in practice.

Second, we share common traditions which, whatever we do at home, we all agree to respect and observe in our everyday encounters. Central to these I would say are our common language, our good manners, our care for children.

We also cherish a tradition of poking fun at politicians, priests and do-gooders, and – though I qualify for mockery on two counts – I think that is a tradition not to be tampered with lightly. And as long as new customs do not conflict with our values, let's embrace them as part of the fabric of our community life. They too will one day join our shared traditions, the outstanding example of course, being the Indian restaurant – now not Indian at all but almost wholly British.

Thirdly, we maintain diverse, individualistic, even eccentric lifestyles in our private lives. No-one tells us how to speak, how to dress, what we should eat or how we should worship. These are all individual choices, to be respected as long as they do not interfere with our fundamental values, or our long-cherished traditions. And unlike some other countries, we tend to embrace new additions to our lifestyle choices – whether it is new music, or new kinds of clothes.

Having set that out, I think we must also be clear that integration has to be a two-way street, in which the settled communities accept that new people will bring change with them. Newcomers realise that they too will have to change if we are to move closer to an integrated society.

We already know a lot about what an integrated society looks like. It has three essential features:

- Equality: everyone is treated equally, has a right to fair outcomes, and no-one should expect privileges because of what they are.
- Participation: all groups in the society should expect to share in how we make decisions, but also expect to carry the responsibilities of making the society work.
- Interaction: no-one should be trapped within their own community, and in the truly integrated society, who people work with, or the friendships they make, should not be constrained by race or ethnicity.

Vocabulary

2 beacon (n.): a good example, a sign of hope – **16 atrocities** (n., pl.): violent and shocking actions involving killing – **18 myriad** (adj.): very many – **25f. to console themselves** (v.): make themselves feel better – **42 to be marooned** (v.): be left in an isolated position – **57 tabloid newspapers** (n.): newspapers, originally the only ones of tabloid size, that concentrate more on popular themes and entertainment than serious news – **71 holy grail** (n.): *here:* ideal solution – **81 to gerrymander** (v.): to change political borders in order to achieve particular election results – **99 to fetch up** (v.): (BrE, infml) end up, get to a place without intending to – **103f. to prize over and above** (v.): think more important than – **120 attachment to** (n.): belief in and loyalty towards – **122 to abide by** (v.): accept and be bound by – **122 notionally** (adv.): as an idea – **127 good manners** (n., pl.): polite ways of behaving, particularly towards other people – **129 to cherish** (v.): think something you have is very important – **129 to poke fun at** (v.): laugh at – **132 to tamper with** (v.): change in a way that might cause damage – **156 outcome** (n.): final result of a process – **165 to constrain** (v.): limit, stop s.o. doing s.th.

Explanations

1 July 6, 2005: the date on which the IOC (International Olympic Committee) announced that the 2012 Olympic Games would be held in London – **13 the days after:** 7 July, when bombs exploded on the London Underground and on a bus, and 21 July, when more bombs in London failed to explode – **23f. the tragedy of New Orleans:** the destruction through flooding and fire of parts of New Orleans by Hurricane Katrina. Poor black people were disproportionately affected. – **58f. the slow massacre of young men and women:** killings of young people in shootings and stabbings

Awareness

1 Do you have friends with other ethnic or cultural backgrounds? Tell the group about your experiences.

Comprehension

2 What events marked July 2005 as special for London?
3 How does the author contrast what happened in New Orleans after Hurricane Katrina with what happened in London after the 7/7 bombings?
4 Why does Phillips think British people might be getting complacent about what happens in the UK?
5 Why does Phillips call the US a 'segregated society' (l. 88)?
6 How does Phillips characterize 'Britishness'?

Analysis

7 Explain how Phillips differentiates between assimilation, multi-culturalism and integration.
8 Explain what Phillips means when he says "integration has to be a two-way street" (l. 148).
9 What sort of speech is this? Compare it with other speeches you know.
10 Explain the allusions in ll. 88–90 and 114–115.
11 Look at l. 96. Explain what 'hyphenated identities' are. What metaphors have been used for the ethnic mix in America?

Opinion

12 Comment on the three features of an integrated society, as the author sees it. For each feature give an example of how that could work in practice, and an example of what would happen if it did not exist.
13 Why did Phillips say Britain might be 'sleepwalking into segregation'? What do you think he meant by this phrase?
14 Compare Phillips' ideas about 'Britishness' with ideas about identity in your own country, e.g. *'Leitkultur'*.
15 What can be said about the report on p. 9 as a reaction to the bombings? What does it reveal about terrorism and ways of opposing it?

Project

16 Find out more about the London bombings of 7/7, the attempted bombings of 21/7, and the shooting of Jean Charles de Menezes.

Internet Project

17 Find out more about the ethnic diversity of London.

"Hatred begets only hatred"*

Twelve days ago, she stood in a London street by the wreckage of the Tavistock Square bus bomb and gripped the world with the power of a grieving mother's words and her call for peace.

"How many mothers' hearts must be maimed? Hatred begets only hatred. It is time to stop this vicious cycle of killing."

Yesterday, Marie Fatayi-Williams stood at a funeral Mass in Westminster Cathedral and offered a simple lament for her only son, Anthony.

"He had promised that when I was little, old and grey, his healthy arms would have been my strength and he would have soothed my pain away. Alas, that was not to be."

She looked towards her son's coffin and broke into song. In the Nigerian Yoruba language she offered a haunting rendition of Auld Lang Syne.

Beside her, Dr Alan Fatayi-Williams, Anthony's Muslim father, and Tom Ikimi, Anthony's uncle and a former Nigerian foreign minister, wiped tears from their eyes.

Marie Fatayi-Williams, however, simply stood red-eyed, but proud.

On July 7, her 26-year-old son, an oil executive, boarded the number 30 bus and was blown up by a fanatical suicide bomber.

Even after the funeral, however, as 700 mourners emerged, many in tears, Mrs Fatayi-Williams refused to give in to anger. "Of course I am sad," she declared. "I lost my only son. I am distraught. I am distraught, but I'm not angry.

"I could be very angry, but if I was angry what would that do? Anger begets hatred, begets more violence, so let's forgive."

Instead, the Mass was a celebration of Anthony as the "world citizen" and friend that he was.

Photographs in the order of service showed a smiling son hugging his mother at a wedding, and grinning again as he placed his hand on the shoulder of one of his sisters. Lauretta, 16, and Ayisha, 13, had left their own tributes in the order of service.

Lauretta's tribute read: "I love you forever and I promise not to be a coconut head. Love you, your 'lulsy-bulbs'."

There was, of course, no hatred at this, the funeral of the son of a Catholic mother and Muslim father. Instead, it was possible to spot the turbans of Sikhs, the saris of Hindus, and Anthony's Muslim friends from Leeds.

Tariq Khan, 32, from Headingley, met Anthony at Bradford University. He was still struggling to comprehend what had happened. "He was a lovely person, the kind that would always break the ice at parties," he said.

In her speech near Tavistock Square, Mrs Fatayi-Williams had vowed: "I am his mother, I will fight till I die to protect him, to protect his values and his memory."

Now, in Westminster Cathedral, Mr Fatayi-Williams, representing the Muslim side of the family, declared that this would be done with the setting up of the Anthony Fatayi-Williams Foundation for Peace and Conflict Resolution. "Anthony was a peace-loving person, and his values we will strive to immortalise."

The congregation prayed for the other victims of the bombings, and also for the bombers themselves. For their part, the churchmen found themselves falling back on the words of Mrs Fatayi-Williams, with Bishop Alan Hopes using her words to urge the congregation not to "yield to the abyss of revenge".

Cardinal Cormac Murphy-O'Connor, the leader of the Roman Catholics in England and Wales, thanked Mrs Fatayi-Williams: "You have spoken of Anthony as a sacrificial victim, whose sacrifice must not be in vain. You have spoken movingly of the need to reject violence, of the obligation to resist hatred and by your words you have set before us all a beacon of light to guide our response to terrorism."

Inside the cathedral, Julie Coker, 65, one of Mrs Fatayi-Williams's regular fellow worshippers at the Church of the Assumption in Lagos – where a simultaneous memorial Mass was occurring – had led the congregation in a lilting African offertory hymn. Now, outside the cathedral she smiled.

"Anthony was a wonderful child. His father is a Muslim, his mother is a Catholic. If the bombers thought they were going to spread hatred, to turn us against each other, they reckoned without Anthony. They reckoned without Marie."

Adam Lusher
The Daily Telegraph,
24 July 2005

2 "Moses in London"*

After the Second World War, Britain's need for labour in post-war reconstruction coincided with economic difficulties in some of its former colonies. The result was immigration on a scale which, though objectively not large, changed the character of British society. Sam Selvon (1923–1994) was born in Trinidad, but his ancestors had been brought to the Caribbean from India by the British to work on the sugar plantations after the abolition of slavery. He lived in London from 1950 until 1978. In his novel *The Lonely Londoners* he describes the experiences of the early West Indian immigrants to Britain in the 1950s. The narrator's use of West Indian dialect adds an element of authenticity to his story. – Sam Selvon, *The Lonely Londoners* (London: Alan Wingate, 1956), pp.7 ff.

One grim winter evening, when it had a kind of unrealness about London, with a fog sleeping restlessly over the city and the lights showing in the blur as if is not London at all but some strange place on another planet, Moses Aloetta hop on a number 46 bus at the corner of Chepstow Road and Westbourne Grove to go to Waterloo to meet a fellar who was coming from Trinidad on the boat-train.

When Moses sit down and pay his fare he take out a white handkerchief and blow his nose. The handkerchief turn black and Moses watch it and curse the fog. He wasn't in a good mood and the fog wasn't doing anything to help the situation. He had to get up from a nice warm bed and dress and come out in this nasty weather to go and meet a fellar that he didn't even know. That was the hurtful part of it – is not as if this fellar is his brother or cousin or even friend; he don't know the man from Adam. But he get a letter from a friend in Trinidad who say that this fellar coming by the ss Hildebrand, and if he could please meet him at the station in London, and help him until he get settled. The fellar name Henry Oliver, but the friend tell Moses not to worry that he describe Moses to Henry, and all he have to do is to be at the station when the boat-train pull in and this fellar Henry would find him. So for old time sake Moses find himself on the bus going to Waterloo, vex with himself that his heart so soft that he always doing something for somebody and nobody ever doing anything for him.

Because it look to Moses that he hardly have time to settle in the old Brit'n before all sorts of fellars start coming straight to his room in the Water when they land up in London from the West Indies, saying that so and so tell them that Moses is a good fellar to contact, that he would help them to get place to stay and work to do.

"Jesus Christ," Moses tell Harris, a friend he have, "I never see thing so. I don't know these people at all, yet they coming to me as if I is some liaison officer, and I catching my arse as it is, how I could help them out?"

And this sort of thing was happening at a time when the English people starting to make rab about how too much West Indians coming to the country: this was a time, when any corner you turn, is ten to one you bound to bounce up a spade.

In fact, the boys all over London, it ain't have a place where you wouldn't find them, and big discussion going on in Parliament about the situation, though the old Brit'n too diplomatic to clamp down on the boys or to do anything drastic like stop them coming to the Mother Country. But big headlines in the papers every day, and whatever the newspaper and the radio say in this country, that is the people Bible. Like one time when the newspapers say that the West Indians think

Early West Indian immigrants

that the streets of London paved with gold a Jamaican fellar went to the income tax office to find out something and first thing the clerk tell him is "You people think the streets of London are paved with gold?" Newspaper and radio rule this country.

Now the position have Moses uneasy, because to tell truth most of the fellars who coming now are real hustlers, desperate; it not like long time when forty or fifty straggling in, they invading the country by the hundreds. And when them fellars who here a long time see people running from the West Indies, is only logic for them to say it would be damn foolishness to go back. So what Moses could do when these fellars land up hopeless on the doorstep with one set of luggage, no place to sleep, no place to go?

Vocabulary

3 blur (n.): s.th. whose shape is not clearly seen – **7 fellar** (n.): (CarE) fellow, man – **17f. he don't know the man from Adam:** he doesn't know the man at all – **20 ss:** abbreviation for 'steamship' – **30 vex** (adj.): (CarE) angry (vexed) – **44 liaison officer** (n.): an official who works with two or more different groups to establish contacts between them and help both sides – **44f. I catching my arse as it is:** (CarE sl.) I'm getting enough trouble in any case – **47 rab** (n.): (CarE) a fuss, trouble – **49 ten to one:** very likely, you could bet on it – **50 bounce up a spade:** (sl.) meet a black person – **54 to clamp down on** (v.): to be more strict with (prevent them immigrating) – **67 hustler** (n.): a person prepared to use any method to sell s.th. or obtain s.th.

Explanations

Intro: The West Indies: the English-speaking Caribbean countries – **6 Chepstow Road and Westbourne Grove:** an area of London in Notting Hill, just North and West of Hyde Park – **7 Waterloo:** Waterloo Station, south of the Thames, is the terminus for trains arriving from the port at Southampton – **8 Trinidad:** island in the West Indies – **37f. the Water:** the Bayswater area of London, North of Hyde Park, between Edgeware Road and Notting Hill – **56 the Mother Country:** Trinidad was a British colony from 1797–1962, other West Indian islands for even longer. Britain was therefore seen as the 'mother country' and often portrayed in this way. Empire and Commonwealth citizens had free right of entry to Britain until 1961.

Info

Us and Them

'Foreigner', meaning a person from another country, usually refers to tourists or visitors.
If a person comes to live in a country, that person is called an **'immigrant'**. People who have been living there for longer, but are identified as belonging to a particular group, are **members of ethnic groups.** **African, Afro-Caribbean, Asian, Australian, German, Polish**, etc. are used to describe these minorities.
People escaping persecution or oppression in other countries are **refugees** or **asylum-seekers**.
People who are not recognized as genuine refugees are sometimes called **bogus asylum-seekers** or **economic migrants**. **Illegal immigrants** are brought in by **people traffickers**.
People who come for a limited period to work are called **migrant workers**.
Xenophobia is a dislike of foreigners. People with this prejudice are **'xenophobic'**. It may express itself in **racial** or **colour prejudice**, or even a whole philosophy of **racism**. A **racist** attitude leads people to **discriminate against** others, or subject them to **racist attacks** or **abuse**.
The aim of the UK government, as expressed through the Race Relations Act 1976, is a just society which gives everyone an equal chance to learn, work and live free from discrimination and prejudice and from the fear of racial harassment and violence.

Awareness

1 What do you know about the 'West Indies', who lives there, and their connections with Britain?

Comprehension

2 Why is Moses going to Waterloo Station to meet someone he does not know?
3 What attitudes does Moses observe in Britain with so many new immigrants arriving?
4 What reason do older immigrants give for not returning to the West Indies?

Analysis

5 'Translate' parts of it into standard English, noting what elements of Caribbean dialect are used.
6 a) Distinguish between author, narrator and protagonist.
b) Comment on the 'voice' of the narrator, as it appears in the descriptions (e.g. of London, Moses blowing his nose, sources of racial tension etc.).
7 What does the text reveal about why immigrants came to Britain from the West Indies, and how they might have been disappointed?

Opinion

8 Moses thinks what the media say is 'the people Bible' (l. 58). How do the media influence what people think and say about immigrants?

9 Comment on the significance of the choice of name for the protagonist.

Internet Projects

10 Find out more about the Caribbean immigrants to Britain ('the Windrush generation').

11 The other main sources of immigration in the 1950s were the Indian subcontinent and West Africa. What sort of people came from those countries, and where did they settle?

12 Where did the people not born in Britain come from? What is the situation in your own country?

Info

Caribbean English

The dialects of Caribbean English as they are used in the West Indies and Britain all differ from one another, but have certain elements in common:

Pronunciation

The words used are English but with African phonetics. This affects nearly all the vowels and certain consonant combinations (th, ng, wn, nt, etc.). Intonation patterns are also different. Within words primary and secondary stress are often placed on different syllables than in standard English.

Vocabulary

The words used are mostly those of standard English, with French influence in some places. A few words have now become obsolete in standard English. Among typically Caribbean words are *vex* (angry), *mash* (break, hit), *duppy* (ghost), *pickney* (child), *tief* (steal), *obeah* /ɒ'beʌ/ (magic, voodoo). Some words are specially Rastafarian in usage, like *ital* /'aɪtæl/ (pure, healthy), or *babylon* (police).

Grammar

There are many grammatical differences in the various dialects. Here are some examples:

Continuous (Progressive) tenses often lack 'to be':
the fellars who coming now

Simple tenses are often replaced by an Infinitive:
Moses Aloetta hop on a number 46 bus

Pronouns have subject forms in the subject of possessive positions and sometimes vice versa:
Ihm ongly doing ihm jab

Object forms are often used as possessives:
Dis ting was yu idea

Subjects may be left out of sentences altogether:
is only logic to say it would be damn foolishness to go back

'So that ...' for purpose is often replaced with 'make + object + do':
You caan turn de light on mek we see?

'Pan' (upon) is often used instead of 'at' or 'on':
doan expect me to come look pan no more house

Plurals are often made by adding 'dem' (them) to the noun:
A not gwine mek no decision til a look pan de inside room dem

'Second-generation' Afro-Caribbean people, who were brought up and educated in the U.K., do not share these dialects to the same extent, usually adopting the language forms of the area they live in.

3 Enoch Powell

"The Birmingham Speech"*

In the 1950s and 1960s immigrants arrived in Britain in considerable numbers from the Caribbean, the Indian subcontinent and Africa, and congregated in particular areas of the country. They encountered racial prejudice from some British people. When Enoch Powell (1912–1998), a Midlands MP and former government minister, warned against the consequences of immigration in a notorious speech in 1968, he claimed to be expressing public opinion, but his views were also widely condemned. – Enoch Powell, "The Birmingham Speech", reprinted in Brian MacArthur (ed.), *The Penguin Book of Twentieth Century Speeches* (London: Penguin, 1993), pp. 377f., 383.

In fifteen or twenty years, on present trends, there will be in this country three and a half million Commonwealth immigrants and their descendants. That is not my figure. That is the official figure given to parliament by the spokesman of the Registrar General's office. There is no comparable official figure for the year 2000; but it must be in the region of five to seven million, approximately one-tenth of the whole population, and approaching that of Greater London. Of course, it will not be evenly distributed from Margate to Aberystwyth and from Penzance to Aberdeen. Whole areas, towns and parts of towns across England will be occupied by different sections of the immigrant and immigrant-descended population. [...]

It almost passes belief that at this moment twenty or thirty additional immigrant children are arriving from overseas in Wolverhampton alone every week – and that means fifteen or twenty additional families of a decade or two hence. Those whom the gods wish to destroy they first make mad. We must be mad, literally mad, as a nation to be permitting the annual inflow of some fifty thousand dependants, who are for the most part the material of the future growth of the immigrant-descended population. It is like watching a nation busily engaged in heaping up its own funeral pyre. So insane are we that we actually permit unmarried persons to immigrate for the purpose of founding a family with spouses and fiancées whom they have never seen. Let no one suppose that the flow of dependants will automatically tail off. On the contrary, even at the present admissions rate of only five thousand a year by voucher, there is sufficient for a further twenty-five thousand dependants per annum *ad infinitum*, without taking into account the huge reservoir

Giles, Daily Express, *27 February 1968*

of existing relations in this country – and I am making no allowance at all for fraudulent entry. In these circumstances nothing will suffice but that the total inflow for settlement should be reduced at once to negligible proportions, and that the necessary legislative and administrative measures be taken without delay. [...]

As I look ahead I am filled with foreboding. Like the Roman, I seem to see 'the River Tiber foaming with much blood'. That tragic and intractable phenomenon which we watch with horror on the other side of the Atlantic but which there is interwoven with the history and existence of the States itself, is coming upon us here by our own volition and our own neglect. Indeed, it has all but come. In numerical terms, it will be of American proportions long before the end of the century. Only resolute and urgent action will avert it even now. Whether there will be the public will to demand and obtain that action, I do not know. All I know is that to see, and not to speak, would be the great betrayal.

Vocabulary

32 funeral pyre (n.): a pile of wood for the ceremonial burning of a (dead) body – **35 spouse** (n.): /spaʊs/ a wife or husband – **35 fiancé** (n.) (fem. fiancée): /fɪˈɒnseɪ/ the person to whom one is engaged (to be married) – **39 voucher** (n.): (BrE) a kind of ticket for a special purpose, (here) quota – **40f. ad infinitum** (adv.): (Latin) /ˌæd ɪnfɪˈnaɪtəm/ without end – **41 reservoir** (n.): a large supply – **43 fraudulent** (adj.): done by fraud, illegally – **45 negligible** (adj.): too small to be worth any attention – **48 foreboding** (n.): a feeling of coming evil – **50 intractable** (adj.): (formal) very difficult to deal with – **54 volition** (n.): choice, without being forced

Explanations

3 Commonwealth: states formerly ruled by Britain. Here Powell means the 'New Commonwealth', i.e. countries whose citizens were mostly black or Asian, who had special rights to enter the UK before it joined the EU. – **7 Registrar General's Office:** government department in charge of compiling population statistics – **13 ff. Margate, Aberystwyth, Penzance, Aberdeen:** towns in, respectively, the southeast of England, West Wales, southwest England and northeast Scotland – **21f. Wolverhampton:** town in the West Midlands, northwest of Birmingham. Enoch Powell was MP for a Wolverhampton constituency. – **24f. Those whom ... make mad:** "Whom Fortune wishes to destroy she first makes mad." Publius Syrus, *Moral Sayings*, 1st century B.C. – **49f. the River Tiber foaming with much blood:** "Bella, horrida bella, et Thybrim multo spumantem sanguine cerno." (I see wars, horrible wars, and the Tiber foaming with much blood) Virgil, *Aeneid*, VI, 86. This quote ensured immediate notoriety for Powell's speech.

Awareness

1 Why are *individual* immigrants often welcomed, while *numbers* of immigrants cause concern?

Comprehension

2 How does Powell arrive at his figures for the year 2000?
3 What sort of immigrants is Powell most concerned about, and why?
4 What dangers does he warn against, and what is his solution?

Analysis

5 Look up the word 'occupy' (l. 16) in the dictionary. What meaning(s) does Powell expect his listeners to associate with it? Find examples where language is used in an emotive rather than factual way.
6 What exactly does Powell mean by 'that tragic and intractable phenomenon' (l. 50) when talking about the US? What assumptions is he making?
7 Analyse what features of the text are typical of a speech and why they are effective for that purpose.

Opinion

8 Comment on Powell's conclusion that 'to see, and not to speak, would be the great betrayal' (l. 60). What do you see as the advantages and disadvantages of expressing an opinion in this way?

9 Compose a letter to a newspaper giving your opinion about immigration to your country.

10 Powell's speech implies that dependants should not be allowed entry. What do you think about treating families in this way?

Project

11 Look carefully at the cartoon on p. 13, noticing its date. Explain the cartoon and comment on its ironies.

Info

Where did they go?

Ethnic groups have often tended to concentrate in particular areas. Suggest reasons for this.

Here are some of the groups in the UK and where they are more likely to be found:

Afro-Caribbeans:	Outer Central London (Notting Hill, Tottenham, Hackney, Clapton, Lewisham, New Cross, Peckham, Brixton, Battersea), Birmingham, Manchester, Liverpool, Coventry, Luton, Watford, Bristol
Arabs:	Central London
Australians:	West Central London
Bangladeshis:	East Central London (Tower Hamlets), Luton, most 'Indian' restaurants throughout UK
Chinese:	Central and East London, Chinese restaurants throughout UK
Greeks/Cypriots:	North London
Indians:	West London (Wembley, Southall, Harrow, Hounslow), Birmingham and the West Midlands, Manchester, Bradford, Leicester, Nottingham, Oxford, Bedford, Slough, Southampton, Thames Estuary
Iraqis:	West Central London, Hull
Iranians:	West Central London
Irish:	North-West London (Kilburn), Liverpool, Manchester, Glasgow
Jews:	North-East London (formerly East Central London)
Pakistanis:	West London (Hounslow), East London (Barking), Manchester, East Lancashire, West Yorkshire, Birmingham, Nottingham, Luton, Watford, Woking, Portsmouth, Cardiff, Glasgow, Belfast
Poles/Czechs:	South-East England, Central Southern England, Midlands (smaller towns)
Portuguese:	East Anglia
Russians:	West Central London
Somalis:	East London, South London (Streatham), Cardiff
South Africans:	North London, West London
Sri Lankans:	East London, South-West London
Turks/Kurds:	North-East London
West Africans:	South London

4

Joan Riley

"Buying a House"*

The statistical data show that certain ethnic groups have tended to congregate in certain areas. One reason is that immigrants tended to seek support from others of their own culture. Another is that racist feelings were often aroused against black or Asian people who tried to move into predominantly white districts. In this extract from a novel by Joan Riley, Adella and her husband, Jamaican immigrants, are visiting a house which is for sale. – Joan Riley, *Waiting in the Twilight* (London: The Women's Press, 1987), pp. 14–21.

The row of houses soared high on either side of the street, testifying to a long-past glory. There was something dark and dismal about them as they clawed their way towards the brilliant blue of the summer sky. Adella had never seen anything so big, so gloomy. Three storeys with cellar and attic, the advert had said. She had looked at the area, had known it would be one of these. She had never been on Eldridge Road before, but it was like any other road in that decaying part of Brixton. "Dese places older dan Granny Dee," she thought with distaste, bitterness creeping into her. All those houses for sale in the paper, neat rows of them filling page after page. How could this one cost so much? She looked pleadingly at Stanton, edging closer to him.

"But dis ting no gwine fall dung?" she whispered unhappily.

Stanton moved away, adjusting his bowtie before throwing her a bitter glance. "Dis ting was yu idea, a doan waan hear bout it," he muttered in irritation. Adella pushed down sudden bitterness. "A know yu tink a wastin de money, but wa yu waan it fa?" she asked angrily. "Is me did earn it. Jesas, Stanton, yu can ongly wear one new suit a time. Yu know why de house important." [...]

The plump, grey-suited man from the estate-agent's office touched her arm, his face red and glowing from the day's heat and his effort at sincerity. Adella looked at her husband, willing him to say something, to assert himself before the other man. Stanton's mouth dropped petulantly, hands jammed in the pockets of yet another new pair of trousers.

"How it cost so much?" she asked finally, realising that she would get no help from him. The estate agent thrust his head forward, looking surprised. Adella stepped back hastily as the sweat running down his face threatened to drip and splash. The grey eyes watching her narrowed, shifted slightly while the smile wavered at the corners. She braced herself for the talk down ways she had come to expect from white people. One thing she had learnt since coming over was that the English looked down on foreigners. It was because of that, that she was determined to get on, to become a success. She was determined to build a better life for the children. The ones back home would get treated like the people coming over to work, there wasn't much she could do about that. But her England-born children would be different. They were going to be just like white people. They were going to be accepted. The man had been casting about for an answer to her question and now his eyes lit up. The mouth extended wider, lips disappearing again into the dazzle of a smile.

"As you can see, madam, it is a big house, he said happily. "The potential is enormous. And the space ..." he tailed off, clutching his file of papers to him as if he could not adequately express the full potential of the place.

Adella gave him a grim smile. She could see the potential all right. That thing was so old, she was sure it would collapse on them if they closed the door too hard.

Tropical products like yams, sweet potatoes and plantains on sale in Brixton

"Dis house look tumbledung," she said accusingly. "How come other one dem soun so better but still cheaper?" "But *are* they better?" the man asked, holding up a finger and arching a brow for emphasis. "Mrs Johnson, I give you my word that you won't get a bigger place." As he spoke he looked significantly at her stomach. Adella spread her hands protectively across the swelling evidence of the new child. She wished Stanton would say something. If only he would stop standing there looking like an idiot and be the man he was always boasting he was.

"Why we caan see one a de other houses?" she persisted. The man laughed uneasily, loosening his tie, as though it was suddenly too tight. "Look, Mrs Johnson, most of those houses, well ... they sell so fast. Many of them are gone before they even reach the papers."

Adella knew he was lying, even without the evidence of shifting eyes and increased perspiration. Some of those houses appeared week after week. She had even taken a bus-ride up the hill to look at some of them. They were nice, those houses. Well painted with neat gardens and pretty gates – those were the sort of houses she had dreamt of owning, *not* this broken-down, half-dead place in the middle of a rotting street.

"What about de one dem dat don't sell?" she insisted, probing at him even while knowing the answer for herself. She wanted to make him uncomfortable, to get back at him for the destruction of her hopes.

The man moved uneasily, the ready smile fading from the red face, replaced by embarrassment. "I am afraid some people are funny about just who they sell their houses to," he muttered apologetically.

She felt her mouth tighten at the evasive answer. Knew what he was really trying to say and she wanted to force him to admit that it was because she was black. "Adella, leave de man alone nuh! Nuting wrong wid dis house." Stanton's hand snaked around her arm as he spoke, clamping down like a vice. Adella felt anger rise as the estate agent lost his harassed air and turned eagerly to her husband, grabbing his words like a lifeline.

"As I was saying, Mr Johnson, it has great potential, and I can see that you are discerning enough to have seen it for yourself."

Stanton nodded, pulling himself to his full height at the flattery.

"With the space this place has got," continued the agent, pressing home his advantage, "you would never have to worry about moving, when your family starts expanding."

"But yu wouldn't live inna it yuself?" Adella interrupted impatiently.

The man seemed uneasy, seeing the sale slip away again. "Me?" he asked in confusion, looking annoyed and upset. "Well ... the truth is ... I mean, I just wouldn't fit into this kind of community. That is to say ..." "A know what yu mean," she said sourly.

Stanton's fingers pinched into her arm. "Leave de man noh," he hissed badtemperedly, "ihm ongly doing ihm jab. Why yu waan trouble ihm?"

Adella ignored him, forcing herself to endure the pain in her arm. "A waan to see de inside," she said with determination. "A not gwine mek no decision til a look pan de inside room dem."

The man looked even more put out. "You must realise that it isn't in the best decorative order," he said hastily, fumbling his slim case for the keys, tongue darting out like a nervous lizard. "You have to look at it from the point of view of its potential. A little paint here and there will soon have it looking great." [...]

After the vivid brightness of the summer sunshine, the house was dark and uninviting. Adella felt the dampness of the place fold around her and seep into her clothes. She moved hesitantly, hands stretched forward, automatically groping in her sun blindness. Her fingers met solid wall, slid into furry coat of spongy dampness. She recoiled, snatching her hand away in horror. The smell of junjo rose to her nose, disturbed by her touch and sudden movement. She had to breathe deeply to steady her nerves, the stale musty air making her uncomfortable. It was like a bad dream and she peered around suspiciously, half-expecting to glimpse something rotting in a hidden corner.

"Yu caan tun de light on mek we see?" she asked suspiciously, only able to make out the faint outline of the two men after minutes in the gloom. Adella pressed closer to her husband, feeling rejected and alone when he moved away.

"I'm afraid I can't use the lights," the agent was saying, "not allowed, you know."

She wondered who didn't allow it. His boss maybe. Not that she blamed them. If she was trying to pawn off something half-dead like this, she would leave the light off too. She supposed it wasn't really the agent's fault. Nobody would want to do what he was doing to them.

"Careful how you go," he said, as he started to lead the way down the long dark passage towards the faint crack of light coming from the outline of a door. "Some of the floorboards are a bit uneven; so if you use your hands to feel your way it will be safer."

Adella ignored him. She was not going to put her hand on that furry fungus-smelling thing again.

The room was big with a high ceiling. Light filtered through the dust of long, wide windows bringing none of the warmth from outside. It was as cold as the passage, and she could see the mildew and junjo growing off the walls.

"But dis place damp," she said.

"No problem, madam, it happens sometimes, you know," the agent confided, eyes wide with false sincerity. [...] "It's been empty a long time," the agent spoke defensively into the silence. "It gets a bit like this, when that happens what with the rain we have been having and all. What it needs is a little heat ..."

A sharp crack interrupted his flow, and Adella saw him lurch sideways, foot disappearing into the stair he had just shifted his weight to. For a moment she stood in stunned surprise, before the meaning of the noise dawned on her.

"De stairs dem rotten," she said accusingly, standing where she was. The man's look of surprise and anger could just be seen in the grey light from an open door above them. His mouth slackened with the beginnings of panic as he swung down on to the next stair, wincing as the trapped foot twisted in the confined space. He tugged at it in alarm.

"What's the matter with you," he asked accusingly, "can't you see me bloody foot's stuck?" [...]

As she walked gingerly down the stairs she thought about her father's house. It was so light, so nice and cool inside. The lacy patterned brick that enclosed the red-polished veranda was always white. Freshly coated with lime it was bright against the lush green vegetation and the red dirt road. Her father was well respected in Beaumont; he had worked hard and bought land, a lot of land. Her mother was a fine dressmaker, and they were comfortable. People looked up to them, asked their advice. They were the envy of the yard. All the children went to school, and her sister Claudia had even gone to Kingston college to train to be a teacher. She felt tears burn at the back of her eyes as she thought of home. If only the money could stretch some more; if only they had saved enough. The child inside her shifted, kicked out, then was still and her heart was heavy with the thought of it. Another child. They could never school them all back home, not if they saved for years. School in Jamaica was too much money. No, they would have to stay in England, till all the children were grown.

She paused at the bottom of the stairs waiting for the agent to catch up with her, ignoring his heavy silence of anticipation. She did not want to see the red and shiny face. The round plumpness of good living and too much beer. [...]

"Doan tell me yu gwine say no." Stanton had come up behind her unnoticed, and impatience showed in his words. "Dis is ten house now yu look at. If yu not gwine tek it, doan expect me to come look pan no more house. A have better tings to do wid my time. And if yu waan know what a tink, if you doan waan buy house, just gi me de money mek me do someting useful wid it."

She bit back her annoyance, moving a little away from him. Stanton was such a disappointment sometimes; and she wondered if they wouldn't have been better off staying in Jamaica. He had been good to her then, not leaving everything, all the planning, all the decisions, on her shoulders. Now she had to make the choice, this house, or the one room where they lived. She supposed he was right. They wouldn't show her anywhere different. She might as well get this one. After all, it was the biggest one she had seen, even if it was no place for invited guests. Other people, West Indians with nowhere to live, relatives, coming up to look for work, they would come. They would probably be glad of a place to stay, and who knows, one day, one day she might be able to buy a proper house. Right now this was the only choice she had.

Joan Riley was born in St Mary, Jamaica in 1959. She now lives in Britain and teaches black history. In 1985 she published her first novel, *The Unbelonging,* which centres on the experiences of a young Jamaican girl coming to England to join her father and his new family; about *Waiting in the Twilight,* her second, she says in the dedication: "This book was written to celebrate the courage and loyalty of one woman and a whole generation of women, who took ship and sailed into the unknown to build a better future for their children. And for the sake of putting at least a small part of the record straight where the West Indian woman in Britain is concerned. To show that the tremendous act of bravery in leaving their home countries and stepping into a society of alien values will not readily be forgotten."

Vocabulary

1 to soar (v.): to rise rapidly or to a very high level - **2 to testify to** (v.): (fml) to show the truth of - **3 dismal** (adj.): causing sadness, gloomy - **3 clawed their way:** climbed, as if with great difficulty - **5 gloomy** (adj.): unpleasantly dark - **13 pleadingly** (adv.): in a begging way - **19 irritation** (n.): anger - **25 estate agent** (n.): (BrE) a person who buys and sells houses for other people - **30 petulantly** (adv.): showing childishly bad temper - **37 to waver** (v.): to be unsteady in movement - **38 to brace oneself** (v.): to prepare o.s. for s.th. unpleasant or difficult - **38 talk down ways:** speaking as if one was more important; patronising, contemptuous - **48 to cast about** (v.): to search or look around - **53 dazzle** (n.): very bright light - **56 potential** (n.): the possibility of developing - **69 tumbledung** (adj.): (CarE) tumbledown, in a condition of near ruin - **100 perspiration** (n.): sweat - **108 to probe at** (v.): to examine (as if with a long metal instrument) - **109f. to get back at** (v.): (infml) to get revenge, punish someone for something bad they have done - **115 evasive** (adj.): trying to hide the truth - **120 vice** (n.): (BrE) a tool used for holding s.th. firmly between metal jaws - **121 harassed** (adj.): made unhappy by troubles - **125 discerning** (adj.): showing an ability to make good judgements - **128 flattery** (n.): insincere praise, given only to gain some advantage - **163 lizard** (n.): a small reptile with four legs and a long tail - **168 to seep** (v.): to make its way gradually through small openings - **171 spongy** (adj.): like a sponge, soft, sometimes wet, not firm - **172 dampness** (n.): slight wetness - **172 to recoil** (v.): to move back suddenly in fear or dislike - **173 junjo** (n.): (CarE) /'dʒʌndʒəʊ/ black or green mould growing on walls - **175 musty** (adj.): with an unpleasant, stale, old smell - **192f. to pawn off** (v.): (infml) to sell s.th. for far more than it is worth - **207 mildew** (n.): a soft whitish or greenish growth on plants, food etc. - **219 to lurch** (v.): to move suddenly to one side - **230 to slacken** (v.): to become loose - **231 to wince** (v.): to make a twisted expression with the face (with pain) - **236 gingerly** (adv.): carefully - **238 lacy** (adj.): like lace (decorative cloth) with holes - **239 veranda** (n.): an open area with a floor and a roof next to a house on the ground floor - **240 lime** (n.): white substance obtained by burning limestone, used in whitewash - **240 lush** (adj.): growing healthily - **258 anticipation** (n.): the act of waiting to guess what will happen - **261 plumpness** (n.): fatness

Explanations

8 Eldridge Road: fictitious road which is, however, typical of many parts of London - **9 Brixton:** an area of South London with a high proportion of West Indian immigrants - **10 Granny Dee:** Adella's old relative at home in Jamaica - **242 Beaumont:** small town in Jamaica - **247 Kingston:** the capital of Jamaica

Awareness

1 What sort of houses do immigrant groups in your country often live in?

Comprehension

2 What makes Adella so disappointed about being shown this house?
3 What advantages of this house does the estate agent point out?
4 What features make the house unpleasant?
5 What reasons does Adella have for taking the house?

Analysis

6 Characterize Stanton and the estate agent. Discuss the differences between what they say and what they think.
7 Look at the use of adverbs in the descriptions of the people and their behaviour. Try to show how emotions are expressed.
8 Look carefully at the use of darkness and light in the descriptions. Comment on how they are used and what effect they have.
9 What becomes clear about the difference between Adella's life in Jamaica and England?
10 Point out where dialect is used in the text, and why.
11 Compare the narration here (e.g. narrative 'voice', use of dialect, point of view) with that in text 2.

Opinion

12 Who in the text are the victims and who are the villains?
13 Comment on Adella's view that "her England-born children would be different" (l. 46).
14 In what ways could this be regarded as a feminist text?

Projects

15 'For Sale' signs are a common feature of English streets. Find out how the British housing market works, and point out the main differences compared with what happens in your country.
16 Try to write a dialogue about the different reactions British people might show if immigrants buy houses in their street.
17 Adella thinks other immigrants with nowhere to live would be "glad of a place to stay" (l. 287). Eventually the house is filled with immigrant families. Find out about the career of Peter Rachman and 'rachmanism'. (You might read the play *Singer* by Peter Flannery.)
18 Read Joan Riley's *Waiting in the Twilight* or one of her other books to find out more about immigrant women in the U.K. and their descendants. Compare it with Andrea Levy's *Small Island.*

5

Linton Kwesi Johnson

"Mekkin Histri"

Linton Kwesi Johnson comes from rural Jamaica, where he was born in a small town called Chapelton in 1952. He came to Britain in 1963 with his mother, who was immigrating to obtain work. He went to school in South London, then, influenced by black writing, decided to say something about his own experiences. The form he chose was 'dub', a poetry backed by music in a reggae style. He became well known in the late 1970s, accepted both by rock music fans (he often performed at concerts) and academics. His work usually appears both on record and in book form. His first LP *Dread Beat An' Blood* (1978) was followed by others including *Making History* (1983). After a gap of several years *Tings an Times* was released in 1991 and the book including these and other poems was published the same year.

now tell mi someting
mistah govahment man
tell mi someting

how lang yu really feel
yu coulda keep wi andah heel
wen di trute done reveal
bout how yu grab an steal
bout how yu mek yu crooked deal

well doun in Soutall
where Peach did get fall
di Asians dem faam-up a human wall
gense di fashist an dem police sheil
an dem show dat di Asians gat plenty zeal

it is noh mistri
wi mekkin histri
it is noh mistri
wi winnin victri

now tell mi someting
mistah police spokesman
tell mi someting

how lang yu really tink
wi woulda tek yu batn lick
yu jackboot kick
yu dutty bag a tricks
an yu racist pallyticks

well doun in Bristal
dey ad noh pistal
but dem chase di babylan away
man yu shoulda si yu babylan
how dem really run away
yu shoulda si yu babylan dem dig-up dat day

it is no mistri ...

now tell mi someting
mistah ritewing man
tell mi someting

how lang yu really feel
wi woulda grovel an squeal
wen so much murdah canceal
wen wi woun cyaan heal
wen wi feel di way wi feel

well dere woz Toxteth
an dere woz Moss Side
an a lat a addah places
whey di police ad to hide
well dare woz Brixtan
an dere woz Chapeltoun
an a lat a addah place dat woz burnt
to di groun

it is noh mistri...

Linton Kwesi Johnson in concert

Vocabulary

Intro/5 dub (n. & adj.): speaking poetry accompanied by reggae music – **5 to keep under heel** (v.): to keep s.o. in a position of subjection and powerlessness – **8 to make a crooked deal:** to have a criminal agreement – **13 zeal** (n.): (usually fml) keenness, energy, courage – **22 baton lick** (n.): (CarE) beatings with sticks carried by the police – **23 jack-boot** (n.): military boot associated with Hitler's armies; the instrument of cruel or Fascist behaviour – **24 bag of tricks** (n.): equipment or techniques used by experts, here: secret or illegal activities performed for a government or other organisation – **37 to grovel** (v.): to lie on the ground, showing extreme respect to s. o. powerful

Explanations

9 Southall: This predominantly Indian suburb of West London was the scene of disturbances when residents and sympathizers opposed the extremist National Front holding a rally in 1979. – **10 Peach:** Blair Peach, a visiting teacher from New Zealand, died during the Southall disturbances after being hit by a police baton. – **26 Bristol:** city in South-West England, where riots began in 1980–81 – **28 Babylon:** Rastafarian word for Western society and the police in particular – **34 right-wing man:** Traditionally, those on the right wing in politics have opposed immigration most strongly. – **41 Toxteth:** Toxteth in Liverpool, Moss Side in Manchester and Chapeltown in Leeds saw serious disturbances in 1981.

Info

Dub Poetry

In the Caribbean, where dub began, words and music have always been intimately connected, for instance in calypso. The poet fulfilled the role of the court jester; poetry was a public and political statement, and music was used to popularize it and make it more acceptable.

In the 1960s, entertainment was provided by DJs with large record collections. Some records were made with a 'dub' side – the vocal track was 'dubbed out' (removed) leaving the instrumental – and the DJ improvised a rhythmic, witty, topical rhyme to accompany it.

Soon poets began to write in a similar way, but allowing the words to carry the rhythm and become the most important element, with the reggae instrumental as accompaniment. The effect was to allow dub poetry to emerge as a serious and expressive poetic style.

In the USA, rap and hip-hop have developed in similar ways to become popular forms of performance poetry.

Awareness

1 What do you know about reggae music, Bob Marley and Rastafari?

Comprehension

2 Listen to the poem/song (Viewfinder Special Audio CD, Langenscheidt ELT 2008, ISBN 978-3-526-51052-9) first without the text, then with it.
3 Try to 'translate' the poem into standard English.
4 Who are the three people the poem addresses? What does the poet accuse them of?

Analysis

5 Explain what the poet is celebrating in each verse.
6 Explain why the poet claims "wi mekkin histri" in the chorus (l. 15 etc.).

Opinion

7 After 1981 the opinions of black people were taken more seriously. The text suggests that resistance – even violent resistance – is sometimes necessary. Would you agree? Explain your view.

Projects

8 Find out more about fusions of music/poetry/politics in reggae or rap in the work of Linton Kwesi Johnson, Benjamin Zephaniah, or American rappers. Try to write and perform a rap or dub poem of your own.

6

"From Riot to Racial Harmony"*

The 'Insurrection' of the 1980s led to important changes in public attitudes towards ethnic minorities. The Stephen Lawrence affair, in which the 1993 racist murder of a black teenager and the dignified struggle over the next 10 years by his parents to obtain justice revealed 'institutionalized racism' in the police force, was another important milestone on the road to ending discrimination. There was also a recognition that some simple changes could produce surprisingly positive results, as on the Broadwater Farm estate. – Cahal Milmo, *The Independent*, 5 October, 2005.

Broadwater Farm today, with green spaces between the concrete blocks

Twenty years ago today, Clasford Sterling awoke to the sound of breaking glass and screaming sirens outside his home on the Broadwater Farm estate. He then witnessed from his balcony the riot which within 48 hours turned 12 low-rise housing blocks in Tottenham, north London, into a byword for urban decay, crime and racial tension in Britain's inner cities.

The youth worker, then 26, had his nose broken by a police truncheon as he tried to calm the rioters amid flying petrol bombs and burning barricades in gloomy car parks that had become the private domains of drug dealers and street robbers.

Today Broadwater Farm – the one-time no-go estate which entered infamy after PC Keith Blakelock was hacked to death during the riot on 6 October 1985 – could hardly be more different. [...]

The transformation of the 21-acre estate, completed in 1970 and currently home to 3,000 people, is on one level purely physical. Gone are the concrete walkways that linked each of the 12 housing blocks above ground in what designers hoped would be a master stroke of social engineering by lifting inhabitants away from cars and roads.

The reality by the early 1980s was less utopian. The walkways formed a warren that could not be policed while the car parks underneath were stalked by crack dealers. Now, each of the housing blocks has a secure entrance hall with a concierge service. Green spaces and play areas punctuate the blocks, renovated at a cost of £33m.

But it is only when its inhabitants talk that the true nature of Broadwater Farm 2005 becomes apparent. Yesterday, a £1m Children's Centre was opened next to its existing community centre and primary school. Jennifer Kamara, 35, a mother-of-four who has lived on the estate for 12 years since coming to Britain from the civil war in Sierra Leone, said: "This is not paradise on earth, we still have the same problems as anywhere else, but people have been given back their purpose and dignity. The kids have their free time occupied and we enjoy the fact that so many different cultures are here. My neighbours are Turkish, my kids walk to school with their Bangladeshi friends. We are one big family on Broadwater."

The statistics prove her point. In 1985, the population of the estate was 49 per cent white, 42 per cent Afro-Caribbean, and 9 per cent from the Indian subcontinent and other areas. Today it is 30 per cent white, 27 per cent west African, principally Ghanaian, 24 per cent Afro-Caribbean and 15 per cent Turkish or Turkish Kurd. A sign at the entrance to the estate says "welcome" in 14 different languages. [...]

Less than a mile from the estate stands the 1,220 pupil White Hart Lane School. Its former pupils include Trevor Phillips. Its former headteacher said it was time to celebrate diversity, not try to quash it. Under multicultural policies such as teaching science in Turkish and implementing special lessons for Caribbean pupils, David Daniels and his team were able to increase the number of pupils passing five or more GCSEs from 10 per cent in 2001 to an expected 50 per cent next year.

He said: "Far from being something which impacts upon UK life I see [diversity] as something that revitalises us and makes us powerful economically."

The extent to which the tensions that sparked events of 20 years ago have eased was demonstrated last month when police raided a suspected drugs den. Chief Superintendent Stephen Bloomfield, the Haringey commander, said: "There was a time when an operation like that would have caused us concern but afterwards the residents came out of their houses and applauded the officers. Broadwater Farm is no longer a place we would consider to be out of the ordinary."

Many outside the Farm do not share his view. Residents complain that taxi drivers refuse to visit the estate after dark and some say they use friends' addresses when applying for jobs.

So it fell to one the estate's oldest residents to explain its new allure. Mary Kemp, 82, has lived on the estate with her husband, Bill, since it was opened. She said: "We moved here from a house with no bathroom. It was like a holiday camp and that remains the case. We are pure English and do you know what that means? It means being tolerant of people, regardless of colour or creed. It means embracing people who are different from you. That's why we stayed here."

Bob Marley, Mahatma Gandhi and John Lennon united on a mural in Broadwater Farm

Vocabulary

Intro/6 estate (n.): a group of buildings planned and built as a unit – **5 low-rise** (adj.): not very tall (opposite of high-rise or tower block) – **6 to be a byword for:** be known as typical of – **6 urban decay** (n.): gradual deterioration of buildings and facilities in part of a town – **14 PC, P.C.:** abbreviation for Police Constable – **19 walkway** (n.): a path to walk along above the ground – **21 master stroke** (n.): a very clever and successful action – **22 social engineering** (n.): changing social behaviour by changing the environment – **24 utopian** (adj.): designed for a perfect world – **26 to stalk** (v.): here: to walk through, causing danger – **26f. crack dealer** (n.): a person selling the drug crack cocaine – **28 concierge** (n.): s.o. who looks after a building and checks on people entering and leaving – **56 to quash** (v.): to stop s.th. existing – **63f. to impact upon** (v.): have an effect on (here negative) – **82 allure** (n.): attractiveness

Explanations

55 Trevor Phillips: a black politician and writer of Guyanese origin; he was Chairman of the Commission for Racial Equality. – **61 GCSEs:** exams in a range of subjects usually taken by pupils at the age of 15 or 16

Awareness

1 Describe any district near where you live which has a large proportion of immigrants.

Comprehension

2 In what ways has the Broadwater Farm estate changed since 1985?

Analysis

3 Why was the Broadwater Farm estate built as is was, what unexpected problems did it have, and what concrete measures were taken to improve things?

4 What does the text reveal about changes in relations between the police and the community?

5 "This is not paradise on earth" (ll. 37f.). – What sort of problems do you think residents still face?

Opinion

6 Comment on what Mary Kemp says.

Internet Project

7 Use the internet to find out more about the murders of PC Keith Blakelock, Stephen Lawrence and Damilola Taylor.

7

"English girl barred from Government job ... because she is wrong kind of white"

Through the use of anti-discrimination legislation like the Race Relations Act of 1976 it has been possible to end overt and covert discrimination in jobs, housing, services and facilities. But attempts to make sure that employment reflects the ethnic diversity of the community have proved more controversial, and fuelled resentment among those who are sceptical about diversity and oppose any further immigration. Stories like the one below are reported in sections of the press as 'political correctness gone mad'. - *Daily Mail*, 6th August 2007.

Daily Mail
TUESDAY, JULY 15, 2008 www.dailymail.co.uk

Abigail Howarth

A teenage science student has been banned from applying for a training programme with the Environment Agency because she is white and English.

The recruitment agency handling the scheme told Abigail Howarth, 18, that there was no point in her submitting an application because of her ethnic background.

But bizarrely she could have applied if she had been white and Welsh, Scottish or Irish.

Abigail, who wanted to join the Agency's flood management programme, saw an advert in a local newspaper offering positions in the Anglia region where she lives, complete with a £13,000-a-year tax-free grant.

It made no mention of the ban on white English applicants, merely noting that candidates from ethnic minorities, such as "Asian, Indian' and "White Other, e.g. Irish, Welsh, Scottish', were encouraged to put themselves forward.

Abigail, of Little Straughton, Bedfordshire, said: "I was really disappointed. To be told being "White English" ruled me out in my home county shocked me. I know why there are positive action training schemes to assist those who are genuinely discriminated against but when it's broken down to this level it seems crazy to me.

"I really wanted to work for the agency and I was very excited - followed by feeling very disappointed.

"I would not have minded had I been beaten for the position by somebody better able than me."

Abigail, who is awaiting the results of A-Levels in environmental science, geography and geology, emailed PATH National Ltd, the company handling applications.

She asked: "Am I correct in assuming that as I am English (White) I need not apply as the preference is for the minorities you have listed, or can I apply anyway?'

Three days later, PATH recruitment officer, Bola Odusi, replied: "Thank you for your enquiry unfortunately the traineeship opportunity in *[sic]* targeted towards the ethnic minority group to address their under representations in the professions under the Race Relations Act amended 2000."

Such a policy may breach Race Relations legislation as employers must prove ethnic groups are under-represented before using positive discrimination strategies.

The Environment Agency admitted it had 'no evidence that white Welsh, Scottish or Irish workers were under-represented' in the Anglia region.

South West Bedfordshire Tory MP Andrew Selous said: "I think this is complete nonsense and the Environment Agency should be taking the best people, irrespective of their background.

"This is obviously borne out of some idiotic quota system. Abigail should have been able to apply and been judged on her own merits. I will raise this when I have a meeting with the Environment Agency next month."

PATH National's organisational development manager, Mary McDowell, said: "The "White Welsh",

"White Irish" and "White Scottish" is a technicality in law – if they are a minority, they are entitled to places on these schemes - they are not part of the majority group, which is "White English".

"The "White English" in this area are the majority group and hence could not apply.

"That is the way the law is laid. This is a chance for

people who might be less employable to gain experience, just experience. Public-sector organisations have a duty to ensure they reflect the make-up of the society they serve."

The Environment Agency says 387 of its 12,000 workers claim BME (Black and Minority Ethnic) status. A spokesman added: "The Commission for Racial Equality has confirmed we are acting legally."

A CRE spokeswoman said: "The Commission will be checking with the Environment Agency to clarify the current situation regarding their positive action initiatives.

"Positive action can only be used to encourage or train particular under-represented groups."

Vocabulary

1 to ban (v.): to forbid – **4 recruitment agency** (n.): a company that finds suitable people to apply for jobs – **8 bizarrely** (adv.): so strangely that it is hard to believe – **13 grant** (n.): money provided for a particular purpose (here to pay living costs) – **39 [sic]** (adv.): the Latin word for 'thus' in square brackets indicates an error in the original text – **40 to address** (v.): do something about – **41 professions** (n.): jobs which need a higher level of education and training – **53 irrespective of** (adv.): without making any differences because of – **79 initiative** (n.): new plan or way of doing s. th.

Explanations

2f. Environment Agency: a body set up to protect the environment and prevent pollution; it has special responsibilities for rivers – **12 Anglia region:** the central area of England – **30 A-Levels:** centralized school leaving exam in Britain, usually in three or four specialized subjects – **41f. Race Relations Act amended 2000:** the original Race Relations Act (law) of 1976 was changed in 2000 to give public authorities a general duty to promote equality – **50 South West Bedfordshire Tory MP:** A member of parliament (MP) in the UK must be elected directly to a geographical constituency, and represents the interests of the voters there. A Tory is a member of the Conservative Party. – **74 Commission for Racial Equality:** the public body responsible for checking that the Race Relations laws are kept.

"I'm so proud to be part of a profession that has never discriminated against women."

Awareness

1 Use role-play situations to simulate discrimination based on random features (hair colour, home district, name, etc.).

2 To what extent do companies, organizations or government reflect the ethnic make-up of the society where you live?

Comprehension

3 What did Abigail apply for, and why was she disappointed?

4 Why does the agency distinguish between different sorts of white?

Analysis

5 Explain the different viewpoints of Abigail, the PATH recruitment agency and Tory MP Andrew Selous.

6 What is the difference between positive discrimination (affirmative action) and positive action? Which is legal and which illegal in the UK?

7 Does the headline of the article accurately reflect the events it describes? What implications can be drawn about the editorial policy of the *Daily Mail*?

Opinion

8 How would you feel if you were Abigail? Write the e-mail she might have sent to one of her friends to describe what has happened.

9 Bearing in mind the experience of discrimination in the US, or the relative positions of women and men in European societies, do you think it would be possible to achieve justice without some form of positive action?

10 In some countries certain positions are only open to state officials, effectively barring immigrants. Do you think there are some jobs which should be reserved for indigenous people in this way?

Projects

11 Find out about the equal opportunities law in your country and compare it with the situation in the UK.

12 Compare this case with other cases of discrimination you have read about / seen in films (e.g. the cricket club that expels Mr Bhamra in *Bend It Like Beckham*, or the night club in *East is East*). What difference would the current legislation make to such cases?

Info

Anti-discrimination laws and 'PC'

The aim of equal opportunities legislation is to prevent people being discriminated against simply because they belong to a particular group. People should have an equal chance to apply and be selected for posts, be trained and/or promoted, and be equally protected from being dismissed without regard to factors such as sex, homosexuality, age, racial origin, religious affiliation, disability or marital status.

Employers can only make decisions on grounds of ability, experience or potential for a particular job. There are two main forms of discrimination:

- **Direct discrimination:** If someone is treated less favourably than someone else, for instance because of their age, colour or religion, or because they come from a different country, or live with a partner of the same sex, get divorced or become pregnant, the employer is breaking the law.
- **Indirect discrimination:** If an employer has a condition that applies to everyone, but some groups are far less likely to be able to comply with it, like demanding British school qualifications or saying that people must be a minimum height, this is also against the law because it makes it more difficult for, in this case, foreigners or women.

'Affirmative action' or 'positive discrimination' (choosing people specially because they belong to a minority group) are not permitted in the UK. However, 'positive action' to encourage or train more members of disadvantaged groups to apply for positions is allowed.

When the first campaigns against discrimination started in the US, they were viewed as 'politically correct', in other words not showing prejudice, which was 'incorrect'. In the 1980s they spread to universities, where attempts were made to open up the traditional canon of literature to include more non-white and women authors, instead of the 'dead white European males' most courses had focused on till then.

'Political correctness' (PC) then extended to reviewing the way history was taught, and laid down 'politically correct' speech and behaviour codes to be used on university campuses. The 'hidden' prejudices of language became a special target, particularly the use of male words instead of general ones, like 'man' or 'mankind' instead of 'human kind'.

In the US, 'affirmative action' was used to give extra advantages to members of minorities or previously disadvantaged groups.

There was soon a backlash, which ridiculed some PC ideas, and it became unclear whether reports that 'short' should be replaced by 'vertically challenged' or 'history' by 'herstory' were serious or satirical.

The term 'PC' is now always used negatively by people who disagree with its aims or regard it as too extreme.

8

Gary Younge

"Mirth of a Nation"

If the Stephen Lawrence case (see Introduction to Text 6) showed that a great deal still needed to be done to improve ethnic relations in Britain, there were more positive signs in the new mixtures of youth culture, in which music, dance, dress and language drawn from the Caribbean, Asian and white communities, with a dash of American hip-hop, became the new mainstream. This new inclusiveness was reflected in the unexpected success of the comedy show *Goodness Gracious Me*. Sanjeev Bhaskar, Nina Wadia, Kulvinder Ghir, and the film-maker and novelist Meera Syal (*Bhaji on the Beach, Anita and Me*) created a show whose title alluded to the stereotype image of Indians portrayed by Peter Sellers in his famous duet with Sophia Loren, 'Goodness Gracious Me'; it questioned all sorts of prejudices and assumptions which communities have about themselves and others, and prepared the way for the even more irreverent humour of Ali G. (DVDs of *Goodness Gracious Me* are widely available.) – Gary Younge, *The Guardian*, 20 February 1999

Peter Sellers portrayed a stereotype of an Indian in his duet with Sophia Loren

Goodness Gracious Me first started to make people laugh on Radio Four in July 1996, and from that moment it became more than just a comedy show. It then transferred to TV and became a display of the self-confidence within the British-Asian population, helping to cement its place at the forefront of the British youth scene. It has now come to illustrate both the symbiosis of Asian and British culture and the resurrection of the politics of humour. And it has revealed the degree to which minority performers must navigate prejudice in their journey towards being accepted by a white majority audience.

It has also created its own genre – "Asian Comedy" – which was previously unheard of in British television. "We weren't sure who our audience would be at first," says Anil Gupta, the show's producer. "You say, 'Asian Comedy', and people say, 'What the hell is that?' It was a bit of a shot in the dark." It was not long until the show was being sold abroad to television stations in Sweden, the Netherlands, New Zealand, Australia, and parts of South-East Asia.

And it has started a debate. *The Times* published a glowing leader, ranking it alongside "comedy classics such as *Yes, Minister* and *Fawlty Towers*", and lauding it as "the oil of race relations". It has won awards from the Commission for Racial Equality and is seen as a welcome triumph for the BBC in its long-vaunted struggle to serve a full cross-section of its licence payers. Several British police forces have asked for permission to use it for teaching race-relations awareness.

But the show has also attracted fierce criticism from some in the Asian community. When it referred to the holy fire at a wedding ceremony as a "fondue", the

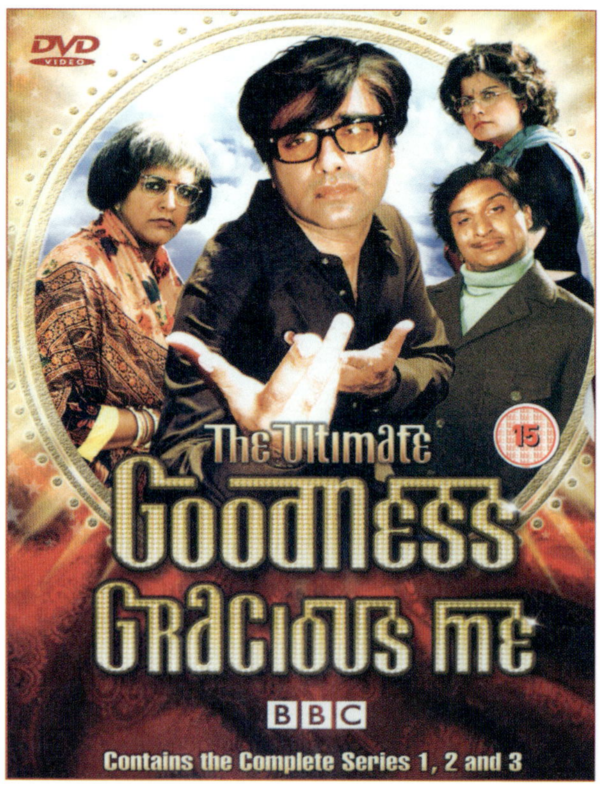

Broadcasting Standards Commission upheld "in part" the complaint of 12 viewers who argued that the "religious symbol of the Hindu faith was unacceptably mocked". "It gives the English the opportunity to laugh at us without thinking about it," says Suman Bhuchar, an independent producer and freelance writer. [...]

"Humour," wrote the Martiniquan poet Aimé Césaire, "alone assures me that the most prodigious reversals are legitimate. Humour alone alerts me to the other side of things." There can be few more prodigious reversals than *Goodness Gracious Me's* best-known sketch – 'Going Out For An English'. The skit involves a group of drunken Asians out at the Mountbatten restaurant in Bombay for an "English". They harass the white waiter and boastfully order the worst food on the menu – "What's the blandest thing you've got?" asks one, and promptly orders 12 plates of chips for six of them.

It is one of several jokes that rely exclusively on the Asian and White-English experience being turned inside out. Others include the Indian students who come to England for a holiday and complain about the beggars and the food, and insist that, if you want to see the real England, you must go to the villages. [...]

There are almost as many views to explain the popularity of the show as there are viewers. Some believe it illustrates the renewed sense of self-confidence among second-generation British Asians. While the first generation of Asians were by no means passive – in the Seventies, they made a stand against race attacks in Southall – their lives were nevertheless informed by their experiences as immigrants who had arrived in Britain to make another life. Their children, who were born and raised here, have both a greater sense of ease, and a keener sense of frustration, about their rights in this country. [...]

Others believe the show illustrates the relatively recent ascent of Asian culture in popular culture generally – the Asian band Cornershop, who made it to number one with their hit record Brimful Of Asha; the trendy Asian Outcaste club and record label; the cropped sari tops in London clubs; the emergence of Brick Lane, at the heart of London's Asian community in the East End, as one of the places to be seen; the bindis decorating the foreheads of Kate Winslet and Madonna. [...]

Its legacy may be that it has transformed the notion that non-white Britons have no popular appeal beyond music and sport. It is the latest, most potent illustration that, with no help from marketing departments, Britain has re-branded itself. With curry as our national dish and clubbers wearing bindis, "white" and "mainstream" are no longer synonymous. Goodness, gracious me.

Goodness Gracious Who?

A guide to [a few of] the show's characters, by Meera Syal

We have collated opinions from three invaluable sources: first, from one of the actresses in the show itself; second, from Dr X, a leading psychologist, who specializes in post-modernist dissection of popular culture, and who has been to Goa twice this year; and last, from Mrs Kumar, who works in a newsagent's in Ilford.

The Bhangramuffins
Two street-wise teenagers who dress in outsize hip-hop wear. Catchphrases: "Kiss my chuddies!" (Kiss my underpants), and "Rasmala!" (an Indian sweet made out of cottage cheese, but here applied to attractive members of the opposite sex.)

Meera: These two characters emerged purely out of observation. You can spot lads like these on most high streets. They dress black, blend rap phrases and Punjabi slang, and spend much of their time trying to be cool and failing miserably (mainly because they both still live at home). Hugely popular, "Kiss My Chuddies" remains the most shouted-out catchphrase in the streets.

Dr X: They obviously represent the collision of second-generation aspiration with first-generation immigrant expectation and tradition. Even their unique language – mother-tongue expletives blended with black street slang – symbolises the new, emerging culture. And all delivered in a strange cockney-Punjabi accent. Their hats are nice, as well.

Mrs K: Hmm, I get these loafer-types in my shop. Let them have their fun, in a few years' time, they'll be wearing suits and married to some good girl known to their families, God willing.

Mr 'Everything Comes From India'
A middle-aged know-all with a patriotic streak, convinced all good and important things originate from India, such as Superman and shampoo. Catchphrase: "Indian!"

Meera: There's a bit of all our dads in this one, or at least the anal, rather shouty uncles we all had, whose attempts to educate us about our wonderful culture generally ended with a xenophobic tirade. He means well, and in his own way, he's an important subversive. After 300 years of colonial rule, why shouldn't we claim a few things back?

Dr X: I was going to say that. Anyway, he proves that appropriation can work both ways, with hilarious results.

Mrs K: He makes me cry. Poor man, obviously missing India so much. And he's right, you know. Harrison Ford's real name is Harijan Firdaus.

The Minx Twins
Two teenage Southall girls, convinced that every man within 10ft fancies them rotten. They invented the term Asian Babe. Catchphrase: "In your dreams, buddy!" and "As if!"

Meera: They were inspired by an article in Minx magazine, in which three so-called "Asian Babes" told how their exotic beauty made men drool and women jealous. (Nothing to do with having massive egos and one collective brain cell, of course.) The actual characters are a lot sweeter, struggling with the dilemma: how can you be a feminist and get a boyfriend?

Dr X: Interesting attempt to demythologise the whole issue of Asian women as dusky bits of Kama-Sutra fodder. Golly, their skirts are quite short, aren't they?

Mrs K: These girls are heading for big trouble. Just give me the names of their parents and I'll do the rest.

Mrs 'I Can Make It At Home'
A killjoy mother, who refuses to spend money on anything, claiming she can Make It At Home For Nothing, usually with the aid of a small aubergine.
Catchphrase: As above.

Meera: This has proved to be one of the most universally recognised characters. Everyone, regardless of culture or race, seems to think she is based on their mother, including us.

Dr X: Beneath the cultural veneer, we share common iconic issues that find a fruitful outlet in humour. Freud called a joke a "pleasure bribe" – our fears made palatable, enabling us to confront them. In a sense, she's everyone's mother, except mine.

Mrs K: What a sensible woman! She should have her own show.

Vocabulary

Intro/4 mainstream (n.): ideas representing the majority of people - **Intro/5 Goodness, gracious me:** old-fashioned exclamation of surprise - **5f. to cement its place** (v.): make sure it is there - **7 symbiosis** (n.): a relationship in which each depends on the other - **17 a shot in the dark** (n.): an attempt to guess s.th. without definite information - **26 long-vaunted** (adj.): praised for a long time, without enough reason - **27 cross-section** (n.): representative group - **33 to uphold** (v.): say it is correct or valid - **36 to mock** (v.): to make fun of, in order to show disrespect - **40 prodigious** (adj.): extraordinary, extreme - **48 bland** (adj.): tasting of nothing - **62 to be informed by** (v.): (usually Passive) to be chiefly influenced by - **65 ease** (n.): being comfortable with a situation, not worried - **72 trendy** (adj.): fashionable, 'in' - **73 cropped sari top** (n.): top in the form of an Indian dress (sari) but leaving the midriff bare - **76 bindi** (v.): (from Sanskrit) dot of colour or jewel worn on the forehead - **80 potent** (adj.): powerful and affective - **82 to re-brand itself** (v.): change people's perceptions about how it is

In 'Goodness Gracious Who?'

3 invaluable (adj.): extremely valuable (here with ironic suggestion of not valuable at all) - **6 newsagent's** (n.): shop selling newspapers etc., typical Asian convenience store - **8 street-wise** (adj.): knowing about how to live in rough areas of a city - **8 catchphrase** (n.): short, well-known phrase made popular by an entertainer or politician - **19 cockney** (adj.): typical of working-class London speech - **20 loafer** (n.): lazy person who should be working - **21 God willing** (expletive): phrase meaning you hope this will happen - **23 streak** (n.): a part of one's character - **25 anal** (adj.): (from Freudian psychoanalysis) showing too much concern for small details - **27 tirade** (n.): long, angry speech - **27 subversive** (n.): s.o. who secretly undermines accepted ideas - **29 appropriation** (n.): stealing s.th. that belongs to s.o. else - **35 to fancy s.o. rotten** (v.): (BrE, infml.) find s.o. extremely attractive sexually - **40 massive ego** (n.): exaggerated idea of one's own importance - **43 to demythologise** (v.): take away superstitious awe of s.th. - **43 dusky** (adj.): poetic word for having a dark or black skin - **44 fodder** (n.): (derogatory) a person or thing only useful for a particular purpose - **44 golly**: old-fashioned interjection to express surprise or admiration - **48 killjoy** (adj.): wanting to spoil other people's pleasure - **56 veneer** (n.): thin layer on the surface of s.th. - **56 iconic** (adj.): *here:* central to one's identity or experience

Explanations

Intro 1 Stephen Lawrence: black teenager murdered in a racist attack in South London (see Text 6) - **Intro 3 Asian:** (BrE) originally from the Indian subcontinent - **Intro 7 Peter Sellers:** British actor and comedian famous for his imitations of voices. In the song he imitates a stereotypical immigrant Indian doctor listening to attractive actress Sophia Loren's heart and using a slightly old-fashioned expression of astonishment. - **Intro 10 Ali G:** creation of Sacha Baron Cohen (see p. 37) - **2 Radio Four:** BBC radio station for news, current affairs, drama, comedy, etc. - **23 *Yes Minister* and *Fawlty Towers*:** Situation comedy shows about the relationship between an incompetent minister and his devious chief civil servant, and a seaside hotel, managed by Basil Fawlty (John Cleese), where everything goes wrong - **24 the oil of race relations:** something which makes races relate to each other more smoothly - **25 Commission for Racial Equality:** an official body designed to tackle racial discrimination and promote racial equality, merging from 2009 with the Commission for Equality and Human Rights - **27 licence payers:** The BBC is funded by a licence paid by everyone with a radio or television; it carries no advertising. - **33 Broadcasting Standards Commission:** one official body which dealt with complaints about radio or TV programmes, replaced in 2003 by OFCOM. - **39 Aimé Césaire:** (1931–2008) poet, playwright and politician from the French West Indian island of Martinique - **61f. race attacks in Southall:** see Text 6 - **70 Cornershop:** indie band from Leicester - **72 Outcaste:** Asian underground club scene and record label which helped make Asian sounds fashionable - **74 Brick Lane:** Bangladeshi area of East London, formerly a Jewish area, which became fashionable from the 1990s; it is the setting for Monica Ali's novel *Brick Lane* (see Text 12) - **82 curry as our national dish:** It has sometimes been said that Chicken Tikka Massala, probably invented by Indian restaurants in the UK, is Britain's most popular dish

In 'Goodness Gracious Who?'

4 Dr X: Meera Syal's humorous mocking of jargon-speaking culture experts who 'know' about India because they have been to the Westernized holiday resorts of Goa. - **5 Mrs Kumar:** Meera Syal plays a similar, but older character in the long-running chat-show *The Kumars at Number 42*, where famous people are interviewed by the Kumar family headed by Sanjeev Bhaskar - **44 Kama-Sutra:** The ancient Indian texts on love and lovemaking (including a variety of sexual positions) became famous in Britain after the translation by Sir Richard Burton was published in the 19th century. It gained a reputation as pornography. - **57 Freud:** Sigmund Freud, the founder of psychoanalysis, wrote about the significance of jokes.

Awareness

1 What comedy shows do you like? Do you know any British comedy shows?
2 If possible, watch a few sketches from *Goodness Gracious Me*.

Comprehension

3 What have been the reactions to the show *Goodness Gracious Me*?
4 What explanations are given in the text for the popularity of the show?

Analysis

5 Comment on the title of the article with its play on words.
6 What does Younge mean by 'the politics of humour' (ll. 8f.)?
7 What examples does Younge give of 'reversal' in *Goodness Gracious Me*?
8 What does Younge see as the significance of the show in modern British society?
9 Look carefully at Meera Syal's guide to the characters in the show. Characterize her three 'experts', showing their stereotypical traits and their use of linguistic register.

Opinion

10 How important do you think it is to laugh at things? Should some things remain sacred?

Projects

11 Find out about the tradition of British radio and TV comedy.
12 Present a British comedy sketch you have found to the group and try to explain its humour, if possible so that it is still funny.

Two sketches from *Goodness Gracious Me*

The Bhangramuffins and football

Bm 1 Are you going to the Old Trafford on Sa'urday?
Bm 2 Of course I'm going, man!
Bm 1 I thought it was sold out.
Bm 2 Tja, man, my Uncle Davinder's a travel agent. He got me one of those sports packages. Includes coach from Southall to Manchester... with a five-day stopover in Wolverhampton.
Bm 1 Does that include match tickets?
Bm 2 *(after a pause)* Bloody Uncle bastard!
Bm 1 Unlucky geezer! Unlucky!
Bm 2 Kiss my chuddies, man! I'll get a ticket at the away supporters' end.
Bm 1 The allocation is sold out!
Bm 2 Man, you're talking about the white man's ticket allocation. There's still the Asian ticket allocation!
Bm 1 What's that, then?
Bm 2 Five per game.
Bm 1 How come there's no more than five Asians at a football match, man?
Bm 2 Ah, the age-old question. The answer is simple. There are two reasons. First of all: ain't no way the Asians are going to eat the crap they serve at football grounds. I mean, I can't see my dad eating no 'meat pie'! Not until they start to define it more clearly. And maybe throw in some coriander, innit?

Bm 1	Good point, man. I mean, I can't see my Auntie Bimla getting her gob round no cold jumbo sausage.
Bm 2	*(looking away in horrified astonishment as the double-entendre dawns on him)*
Bm 1	*(after a pause, as it dawns on him too)* What, what, what, what, what's the second reason, man?
Bm 2	The second reason is this, right? If you go to football every Saturday, who's going to look after the shop?
Bm 1	Yeah, I never thought of that! So, who did you support in the World Cup?
Bm 2	What're you on about now?
Bm 1	I mean, did you support England, or did you support France 'cos they won?
Bm 2	Man, that is a stupid question! There was only one team to support! The team that represents the motherland of our culture, our language, our way of life!
Bm 1	India weren't there, man!
Bm 2	Not India! I'm talking about Jamaica!

Mr 'Everything Comes from India' and the Royal Family

The father is watching television with his son

Son:	Ah, Trooping of the Colour! Great! The Queen looks nice, doesn't she?
Father:	Nice? Of course nice! Because she's Indian!
Son:	Not the Queen!
Father:	All of them, the whole Royal family, Indian!
Son:	What'ya talking about?
Father:	Uh? Think about it, yaar. Descended from Queen Victoria, Empress of India, so Indian!
Son:	Rubbish!
Father:	Not rubbish. Look at them. They all live in the same family house together. Indian! All work in the family business. Indian! All have arranged marriages. Indian! They all have sons. Daughters no good. Indian!
Son:	But Dad...
Father:	Children live with their parents until they're married. Indian!
Son:	Dad, Dad...
Father:	What more do you want? Do you want them to put on turbans and charm snakes out of baskets?
Son:	But Dad, Harry, Wills, Fergie...
Father:	All Indian! All except Prince Charles. He's African.
Son:	What?
Father:	If he was Indian, he'd have smaller ears!

Vocabulary

2 Bhangramuffin (n.): word combining 'bhangra', a Punjabi musical style, with 'raggamuffin', a Jamaican city boy (see also Text 5) **13 geezer** (n.): (infml) cockney word for man – **14 away supporters** (n.): fans of the team not at home in this stadium – **15 allocation** (n.): number reserved for a particular group – **22 crap** (n.): literally excrement; *here:* rubbish – **24 coriander** (n.): (BrE) a herb frequently used in Indian cuisine – **24 innit?:** (urban youth sl.) all-purpose question tag – **25 gob** (n.): (sl.) mouth – **25 jumbo** (adj.): very big – **27 double-entendre** (n.): word or phrase which can be understood in two ways, one often sexual – **27 to dawn on** (v.): when an idea comes to you slowly – **48 yaar (n.):** Hindi / Urdu word when talking to s.o., like 'man'

Explanations

2 Old Trafford: the Manchester United football stadium – **10 Wolverhampton:** industrial town near Birmingham with a large Asian population – **42 Trooping the Colour:** a military parade held every year in June to mark the Queen's official birthday – **48 Empress of India:** the title created for Queen Victoria in 1876 – **58 Harry, Wills, Fergie:** nicknames of Prince Harry and Prince William, the sons of Prince Charles, and Sarah Ferguson, the red-haired former wife of Prince Andrew

TASKS

In the Bhangramuffin sketch:

1 What are the drawbacks about the uncle's offer?
2 Why might an Indian be reluctant to eat a 'meat pie'?
3 What does the sketch reveal about identity?

In the 'Everything comes from India' sketch:

4 How are stereotypes about India used?
5 What is the fact on which the punch-line depends?
6 Try to write your own sketch (on any subject) ending with a punch-line.

9 Gurinder Chadha

"Going for Goal"*

Jesminder (Jessie) Bhamra is a passionate footballer, whose greatest ambition is to play as a professional with skills like her idol, David Beckham, renowned for bending the ball past defenders. However, as a girl, and as a Sikh, whose families have strict ideas about their daughters' upbringing, she has a problem. Her parents want her to study to be a lawyer or a doctor, and forbid her to continue playing in her local Hounslow team. Gurinder Chadha, who wrote and directed the movie *Bend It Like Beckham*, has not always found it easy to be a Punjabi woman film-maker. – *Bend It Like Beckham* (film released in 2002).

"I played in the final today, and we won!"

Jesminder: How am I going to tell them, Tony? I'll have to now or I'll end up a solicitor, bored out of my mind.

Tony: Come with me. (*They go into the living-room*) Mum, Uncleji, Auntieji, we've got something we want to tell you.

Aunt Biji: Why is he holding her hand?

Tony: We've been good friends for a long time now. We'd like to ask for your blessings.

(*All look puzzled*)

We'd like to get engaged.

(*Exclamations in Punjabi*)

But look, there's one condition: I want Jesminder to go to college first, anywhere that she wants.

Mr Bhamra: Of course, putar. (*He congratulates Tony*)

Mrs Bhamra: Well, we have relatives all the way, in Glasgow, in Portsmouth ...

(*Embraces*)

Jesminder: Mum, Dad ... Tony's lying.

Voice: Lying?

Jesminder: We're not getting married. Tony only said that to help me, but I'm not lying any more. I played in the final today, and we won!

Mrs Bhamra: How? When?

Jesminder I wasn't going to go, but Dad let me. And it was brilliant! I played the best ever! And I was happy because I wasn't sneaking off and lying to you! I didn't ask to be good at football. Guru Nanak must have blessed me. Anyway, there was a scout from America there today, and he's offered me a place at a top university with a free scholarship and a chance to play football professionally, and I really want to go, and if I can't tell you what I want now, then I'll never be happy, whatever I do.

Mrs Bhamra: You let her leave her sister's wedding to go to a football match?!

Mr Bhamra: Maybe you could handle her long face; I could not. I didn't have the heart to stop her. (*gets up and moves towards the bar*)

Mrs Bhamra: And that's why she's ready to go all the way to America now!

Bubbly: (*whispering and gesturing*) She's dead, man.

Tony: (*to his mother*) It's allright, Mum, just leave it.

Mr Bhamra: (*pouring himself a glass of whisky*) When those bloody English cricket players threw me out of their club, like a dog, I never complained. On the contrary, I vowed that I will never play again. Who suffered? Me. But I don't want Jessie to suffer. (*Jesminder sheds a tear*) I don't want her to make the same mistakes that her father made of accepting life, accepting situations. I want her to fight. And I want her to win... because I've seen her play and she's, she's brilliant! I don't think anybody has the right of stopping her. (*Jesminder embraces him*) Two daughters made happy in one day. What else can a father ask for?

Mrs Bhamra: At least I've taught her full Indian dinner. The rest is up to God. (*Laughter*)

Vocabulary

2 solicitor (n.): a lawyer who gives legal advice to people – **16 putar** (n.): Hindi / Punjabi word meaning son (or daughter)

Explanations

5 uncleji: In Indian English the parents of friends are often called 'aunt' and 'uncle'. The suffix -ji is added as a sign of respect and affection. – **31 Guru Nanak:** Guru Nanak Dev (1469–1539) was the founder of the Sikh religion. A picture representing him hangs on the wall in the Bhamras' house. – **53 those bloody English cricket players:** Mr Bhamra explained earlier in the film how he had been a good cricketer in East Africa, where he used to live, but in England the local cricket club refused to admit a non-white player.

Awareness

1 Do you know any cases where parents quarrelled with their children about what they wanted them to do or be?

2 Find out from the internet about the main principles of the Sikh religion, in particular the teachings of the gurus and the '5 Ks'. You could start at www.sikhs.org.

Comprehension

3 Why does Tony announce that he and Jesminder are engaged?

4 What two other things have happened on this day?

5 Why does Bubbly (a friend of Jesminder's sister's, also grown up in a Sikh family) say what she does?

Analysis

6 How do Mrs Bhamra's words reveal the attitudes of traditionalist Sikh women?

7 What differences in speech can be observed between the older and younger generations?

8 In what ways is Mr Bhamra not a good Sikh?

Opinion

9 Is Mr Bhamra's agreement a decision to reject his traditional values? Explain your opinion.

Internet Projects

10 Use the internet to find out more about the part of London near Heathrow airport (where the film is set) and the ethnic groups that live there.

11 Compare this with another film on similar themes, like *East is East,* or *What's Cooking*?

12 Gurinder Chadha is a successful film director. Find out about other successful Indians in the UK.

10

Gautam Malkani

"Names"*

In the 1970s white racist 'skinhead' gangs regularly went 'Paki-bashing': insulting and beating up Asians (people from the Indian subcontinent), because they thought they would not fight back. In the novel *Londonstani,* set in contemporary Hounslow, the situation is very different. Gautam Malkani, its author, was born in 1976, grew up near Heathrow Airport and works as a journalist. – Gautam Malkani, *Londonstani* (London: Fourth Estate, 2006), pp. 33 ff.

– Serve him right he got his muthafuckin face fuck'd, shudn't b callin me a Paki, innit.

After spittin his words out Hardjit stopped for a second, like he expected us to write em down or someshit. Then he sticks in an exclamation mark by kickin the white kid in the face again. – Shudn't b callin us Pakis, innit, u dirrty gora.

Again, punctuation came with a kick, but with his left foot this time so it was more like a semicolon. – Call me or any a ma bredrens a Paki again an I'ma mash u an yo family. In't dat da truth, Pakis? – Dat's right, Amit, Ravi an I go, – dat be da truth.

The three a us spoke in sync like we belonged to some tutty boy band, the kind who sing the chorus like it's some blonde American cheerleader routine. Hardjit, Hardjit, he's our man, if he can't bruckup goras, no one can. Ravi then delivers his standard solo routine: – Yeh, blud, safe, innit.

– Hear wat my bredren b sayin, sala kutta? Come out wid dat shit again n I'ma knock u so hard u'll b shittin out yo mouth 4 real, innit, goes Hardjit, with an eloquence an conviction that made me green with envy. Amit always liked to point out that brown people don't actually go green: – We don't go red when we been shamed an we don't go blue when we dead, he'd said to me one time. – We don't even go purple when we been bruised, jus a darker brown. An still goras got da front to call us coloured.

It was an old joke but, green or not, I in't shamed to admit I'm envious a Hardjit. Most bredren round Hounslow were jealous a his designer desiness, with his perfectly built body, his perfectly shaped facial hair an his perfectly groomed garms that made it look like he went shopping with P Diddy. Me, I was jealous a his front – what someone like Mr Ashwood'd call a person's linguistic prowess or his debating dexterity or someshit. Hardjit always knew exactly how to tell others that it just weren't right to describe all desi boys as Pakis. [...] People're always tryin to stick a label on our scene. That's the problem with havin a fuckin scene. First we was rudeboys, then we be Indian niggas, then rajamuffins, then raggastanis, Britasians, fuckin Indobrits. These days we try an use our own word for homeboy an so we just call ourselves desis but I still remember when we were happy with the word rudeboy.

"Designer desiness": Sacha Baron Cohen, as 'Ali G', made fun of urban youth culture in various media shows and films

Vocabulary

2 innit: (isn't it?): (urban sl.) all-purpose question tag – **7 gora** (n.): Hindi / Punjabi for a white person – **10 bredrens** (n.): Jamaican English / Rastafarian word for brothers – **11 to mash** (v.): (CarE) to squash, beat up – **14 tutty** (adj.): (urban sl.) low-quality, dirty – **16 bruckup** (v.): (CarE) beat up – **18 blud** (n.): (urban sl.) mate, friend (from Jamaican and US usage) – **18 safe** (adj.): (urban sl.) all right – **19 sala kutta:** Hindi / Punjabi insult: stupid dog or stupid ox – **28 front** (n.): (urban sl.) effrontery, cheek – **31 desiness** (n.): /'deɪsɪ'nɪs/ being a 'desi' (from Sanskrit 'from the Mother Country') – **33 garms** (n.): (urban sl.) clothes (from garments)

Explanations

3 Hardjit: The narrator's friend Harjit has changed his name to express his hardness – **34 P Diddy:** American record-producer and rapper Sean John Combs, born 1969, previously known as Puff Daddy, is also a clothing designer. – **35 Mr Ashwood:** the narrator's favourite teacher at college

Awareness

1 Give some examples of how young people use language that older people might not understand or approve of.

Comprehension

2 What is Hardjit doing, and why?

Analysis

3 Investigate and comment on the use of language and try to 'translate' it into standard English.
4 In what ways does the narrator seem to use language differently? What might this suggest about him?
5 What different cultural ingredients can be found in this passage?

Opinion

6 What is ironic about Hardjit's actions?
7 What do you think makes a person 'cool'?

Projects

8 Find out about the meanings and origins of the terms 'rudeboys', 'niggas', 'rajamuffins', 'raggastanis', 'Britasians', 'Indobrits' and 'desis'.
9 Explore the dictionary of urban slang at www.urbandictionary.com.
10 Compare this scene with either Anthony Burgess's *A Clockwork Orange* or Irvine Walsh's *Trainspotting*.

11 Xiaolu Guo

"Home"

There has been a Chinese community in Britain for a very long time. In the 20th century many Chinese sailors settled in seaport towns like London, Liverpool or Southampton. They often started laundry businesses. Later Chinese restaurants and takeaways opened all over the country. After the Communists took power in China, most Chinese immigration was from Hong Kong. Now Chinese students, and students from all over the world, come to the UK on limited visas to learn English and study at British universities. Xiaolu Guo is a writer and film-maker who writes in Chinese and English. Her novel *A Concise Chinese-English Dictionary for Lovers*, written in the form of a diary under headings of definitions of words, describes the year a student called 'Z' spends in London, discovering differences in culture and learning about love with the Englishman she has moved in with. – Xiaolu Guo, *A Concise Chinese-English Dictionary for Lovers* (London: Chatto & Windus, 2007), pp. 123–126

home n place where one lives; institution for the care of the elderly, orphans, etc *adj* of one's home, birthplace, or native country; sport played on one's own ground

'I am going to go to see a family nearby, do you want to come?' you ask me.

'Family? What kind of family? Not your family?'

'No. They are Bengalis.'

Is not very normal you want see other family. Because you not really like family concept. You say family against community. You say family is a selfish product.

It seems that you like other's family more than you like your own. In this Bengali family, you know those kids for many years, since you worked as youth worker. In a house, between Brick Lane and Bethnal Green Road, old Bengali mother raises ten children. Is big three-floor house with ten little rooms. Five childrens are from same mother, and another five childrens are from another woman but with the same man. The father, a Bengali married man, came to London twenty-five years ago and remarried to this mother in London. He ran some business between England and Bangladesh. Then he died, left one family in London, one family in Bangladesh. But the five Bangladesh-living children want come to London, so they were brought here living with this London mother. These kids are from three to twenty-four. The youngest one was born in 2000. How strange a child born of that year! He only can say 'bye-bye' in English. The oldest one just graduated from the Gold Smith College. He studied Politics and he wants become lawyer.

'I not understand how mother can raise ten children without a husband,' I say in little voice. 'And she doesn't have any job either!'

'That's why I like this family. They just get on with their life without making any fuss. They have a small business making earrings and necklaces from home.'

'And two groups of children from different mother, they don't fight at all?'

'No. They enjoy sharing life together, not like other families. I wish my family was like this.'

'Do you hate your family?' I ask.

'Well, I don't like them. They are sad people. I broke away from them many years ago.'

You go into silent.

I can't imagine what like to break up with my family. Even though my mother very bad temper and make me pain, my life relies on them, and I can't survive without them.

'Do you want have family with me?' I ask.

'Aren't we a family now?' you say.

'No, a real family.'

'What is a real family?'

'House, husband and wife, then have some children, then cooking dinner together, then travel together ...'

'I thought the Chinese were supposed to be Communists.'

You seem like making fun. What you mean?

We look at each other, no more discussion on this.

You say *salaam malai coom* to the old mother. The mother, she is covered in old green Sari. Her skin is deep brown and lots of wrinkles on her face. She never any education and never speak one word English. She always smiles and very little talking. When her children talks in English loudly in TV room and watching BBC she just sit there, peacefully watching, like she understand they say. Bathroom flush doesn't work and shower doesn't work. There is not money to fix house. But it seem fine for them. It seem their life is not messy at all. They use cold-water shower once a week, and they don't use toilet paper because they always use water to clean then tip bucket down loo.

There are drug dealers doing business outside of their windows, and many drunkens pass by with bottles clunkling every night, but the family not get any harm.

In Chinese, it is the same word (jia) for 'home' and 'family' and sometimes including 'house'. To us, family is same thing as house, and this house is their only home too. [...]

But English, it's different. In *Roget's Thesaurus*, 'Family' related to: *subdivision, greed, genealogy, parental, posterity, community, nobility.*

It seems like that 'family' doesn't mean a place. Maybe in West people just move round from one house to another house? Always looking for a house, maybe that's the lifelong job for Westerners.

I keep telling you I need a home. Your face look gloomy, and seem disappointed that you cannot make me happy.

'But I am your home,' you say.

'Yes, but you always move around, and you don't want live in this house.'

'You're right. I'm tired of living in the city.' Then you add, 'I can't see myself getting married either.'

'But I like city and like to have marriage. So that mean we can't have a home together,' I confirm.

'No, I didn't say that,' you say.

You look distant to me.

Vocabulary

39 sad (adj.): to be pitied, lonely, not having fun – **68 salaam malai coom:** (usually Salaamu Alaykum) universal greeting in Muslim countries, meaning 'Peace be upon you' – **75 flush** (n.): the part of a toilet that cleans it with a sudden flow of water – **83 clunkling:** the narrator's misspelling of clunking (making the noise of bottles hitting each other)

Explanations

4 Bengalis: people from the area called Bengal, at the mouth of the Ganges, now divided between India and Bangladesh – **11 Brick Lane:** Bangladeshi area of East London; it is the setting for Monica Ali's novel *Brick Lane* (see Text 12) – **11f. Bethnal Green Road:** the road at the northern end of Brick Lane – **26 Gold Smith College:** Goldsmiths College, part of the University of London, situated in south-east London – **88 *Roget's Thesaurus*:** a reference work consisting of lists of related words divided into categories, first collected by Dr Roget in the early 19th century. There are now different versions, and the thesaurus is commonly used by people who write in English to find the exact word they are searching for.

Awareness

1 What do you know about China and its history, and the relations between China and Britain?
2 What can you find out about the Brick Lane district of London and its history?

Comprehension

3 Who does the narrator address as 'you'?
4 What does the reader learn about the Bengali family and their life in England?
5 What are the main differences between the English and Chinese ideas of 'home' and 'family', according to the narrator?

Analysis

6 Analyse how the author uses language, and suggest reasons for what she has done.
7 'Translate' passages of 'Chinese English' into standard English.
8 Look up the definitions of the words the narrator finds in *Roget's Thesaurus* in your dictionary. What ideas and connotations about 'family' do they convey?
9 What hinders the narrator and the man she talks to from being a family?
10 Why do you think the author has chosen the word 'home' as the title of this entry?

Opinion

11 Do you think the Bengali family is to be pitied or envied?

12 Assess the evidence from the text suggesting whether or not the gulf between cultures is unbridge-able?

Projects

13 Find and learn how to use *Roget's Thesaurus*. Compare it with the thesaurus function on a word-processing program.

14 What opportunities are there for foreign students to study in the UK? Use the Internet to find out about some of the courses and programmes available, and what they cost.

15 Find out about other Chinese or Chinese-British writing in English, for example by Timothy Mo or Jung Chang.

12 Monica Ali

"The Immigrant's Tragedy"*

Bangladesh, formerly East Pakistan, has been an important source of immigration to the UK. Most 'Indian' restaurants scattered throughout the country are in fact run by families from Bangladesh. In London, Bangladeshi immigrants settled in the East End, in an area previously known for its poor Jewish immigrant population. Monica Ali (b. 1967) set her first novel *Brick Lane* in the area, with its Bengali street signs, garment workshops, restaurants and shops. The novel, shortlisted for the Man Booker Prize, was an immediate bestseller, although some within the Bangladeshi community objected to the way they were portrayed in it. The book centres on Nazneen, a woman sent from Bangladesh to marry a much older man, Chanu, whose plans are always grander than his achievements. In this extract, Chanu has brought Nazneen and baby Raquib to his friend Dr Azad's flat, although the doctor has not invited them. There they meet Mrs Azad for the first time. – Monica Ali, *Brick Lane* (London: Doubleday, 2003), pp. 112ff.

Mrs Azad switched off the television. Let's go, thought Nazneen. She tried to signal with her eyes to Chanu, but he smiled vaguely back at her. 'This is the tragedy of our lives. To be an immigrant is to live out a tragedy.'

The hostess cocked her head. She rubbed her bulbous nose. 'What are you talking about?'

'The clash of cultures.'

'I beg your pardon?'

'And of generations,' added Chanu.

'What is the tragedy?'

'It's not only immigrants. Shakespeare wrote about it.' He cleared his throat and prepared to cite his quotation.

'Take your coat off. It's getting on my nerves. What are you? A professor?'

Chanu spread his hands. 'I have a degree in English Literature from Dhaka University. I have studied at a British university – philosophy, sociology, history, economics. I do not claim to be a learned gentleman. But I can tell you truthfully, madam, that I am always learning.'

'So what are you then? A student?' She did not sound impressed. Her small, deep-plugged eyes looked as hard and dirty as coal.

'Your husband and I are both students, in a sense. That's how we came to know each other, through a shared love of books, a love of learning.'

Mrs Azad yawned. 'Oh yes, my husband is a very refined man. He puts his nose inside a book because the smell of real life offends him. But he has come a long way. Haven't you, my sweet?'

He comes to our flat to get away from her, thought Nazneen.

'Yes,' said the doctor. His shirt collar had swallowed his neck.

'When we first came – tell them, you tell them – we lived in a one-room hovel. We dined on rice and dal, rice and dal. For breakfast we had rice and dal. For lunch we drank water to bloat out our stomachs. This is how he finished medical school. And now – look! Of course, the doctor is very refined. Sometimes he forgets that without my family's help he would not have all those letters after his name.'

A corner of Brick Lane, where the street names are in Bengali and English

'It's a success story,' said Chanu, exercising his shoulders. 'But behind every story of immigrant success there lies a deeper tragedy.'

'Kindly explain this tragedy.'

'I'm talking about the clash between Western values and our own. I'm talking about the struggle to assimilate and the need to preserve one's identity and heritage. I'm talking about children who don't know what their identity is. I'm talking about the feelings of alienation engendered by a society where racism is prevalent. I'm talking about the terrific struggle to preserve one's sanity while striving to achieve the best for one's family. I'm talking –'

'Crap!'

Chanu looked at Dr Azad but his friend studied the backs of his hands.

'Why do you make it so complicated?' said the doctor's wife. 'Assimilation this, alienation that! Let me tell you a few simple facts. Fact: we live in a Western society. Fact: our children will act more and more like Westerners. Fact: that's no bad thing. My daughter is free to come and go. Do I wish I had enjoyed myself like her when I was young? Yes!'

Mrs Azad struggled out of her chair. Nazneen thought – and it made her feel a little giddy – *she's going to the pub as well*. But their hostess walked over to the gas fire and bent, from the waist, to light it. Nazneen averted her eyes.

Mrs Azad continued. 'Listen, when I'm in Bangladesh I put on a sari and cover my head and all that. But here I go out to work. I work with white girls and I'm just one of them. If I want to come home and eat curry, that's my business. Some women spend ten, twenty years here and they sit in the kitchen grinding spices all day and learn only two words of English.' She looked at Nazneen who focused on Raqib. 'They go around covered from head to toe, in their little walking prisons, and when someone calls to them in the street they are upset. The society is racist. The society is all wrong. Everything should change for them. They don't have to change one thing. That,' she said, stabbing the air, 'is the tragedy.'

Vocabulary

Intro/7 to shortlist (v.): to put s. o. on a shorter list from which the winner is chosen – **3 vaguely** (adv.): in a way that shows he is not concentrating – **5 to cock** (v.): to hold at an angle – **5 bulbous** (adj.): large and round – **7 clash** (n.): conflict arising out of differences – **18 learned** (adj.): /lɜːnt/ having studied and gained a lot of knowledge – **22 deep-plugged** (adj.): set deep in the face – **27 to yawn** (v.): to open your mouth wide and breathe deeply, often as a sign of boredom or contempt – **28 refined** (adj.): well-educated, and thus of a higher social class – **36 hovel** (n.): a small, dirty place to live – **36 dal** (n.): Indian dish like thick soup made with lentils – **39 to bloat** (v.): to fill up (so that you feel you have eaten too much) – **55f. heritage** (n.): traditional beliefs, values and customs – **59 alienation** (n.): feeling cut off from a group – **59 to engender** (v.): to cause – **60 prevalent** (adj.): common, widespread – **61 sanity** (n.): being mentally healthy – **63 crap** (n.): (rude word, originally meaning excrement) rubbish, nonsense – **77 giddy** (adj.): feeling unsteady and unable to balance properly – **79 gas fire** (n.): old-fashioned heater with gas-jets heating ceramic elements – **81 to avert** (v.): to turn away

Explanations

16 Dhaka: the capital of Bangladesh – **16f. studied at a British university:** Chanu is doing a course with the Open University, which teaches via radio and television and work is sent in by post or e-mail.

Awareness

1 What is normally understood by the terms 'clash of cultures' and 'second-generation immigrants'? Distinguish between 'clash of cultures' and 'clash of civilizations'.
2 If you emigrated to another country, how much of your culture would you wish to keep? How much would you want to pass on to your children?

Comprehension

3 Who takes part in the conversation?

Analysis

4 Analyse and compare the two views of the immigrant's tragedy presented here.
5 Determine the narrative point of view. What does the reader learn about Nazneen and her way of life?
6 Why does Dr Azad say so little? What can the reader infer from this?
7 Why does Nazneen feel 'giddy' (l. 77)?
8 What seems to be Mrs Azad's view of education?

Opinion

9 Who does the reader sympathize with more, Chanu or Mrs Azad? Which opinions is the reader more likely to agree with? What is the effect of this narrative technique?

Projects

10 'Shakespeare wrote about it.' (l. 11). Try to discover where Shakespeare wrote about the problems of different generations or of minorities, and present your findings to the group.
11 Use internet resources to try to make a 'country profile' of Bangladesh and suggest why people might want to emigrate from it.
12 Find out what dishes might be on the menu in a typical Bangladeshi restaurant in the UK.

13

Hanif Kureishi

"My Son the Fanatic"

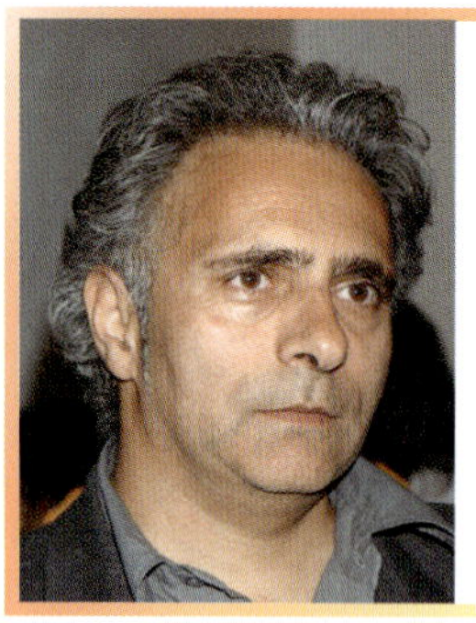

Hanif Kureishi's father was a Muslim from Bombay (his family moved to Pakistan after Indian independence) and his mother English. Born in 1954 in South London, Kureishi grew up very much aware of the racial and cultural tensions experienced by immigrants, but refused to be determined by them. His novels, stories and film screenplays often show uncanny sensitivity to the times. His screenplay *My Beautiful Laundrette* (available in Viewfinder Literature) was a surprise mainstream success. The story from which this extract is taken was also made into a feature film starring Om Puri as Parvez. – 'My Son the Fanatic', in *Love in a Blue Time* (London: Faber & Faber, 1997), pp. 124ff.

The next day, Parvez went immediately to the street where Bettina stood in the rain wearing high heels, a short skirt and a long mac on top, which she would open hopefully at passing cars.

'Get in, get in!' he said.

Bettina put her arms around him.

'What's happened?'

'I've just had the worst experience of my life.'

As Bettina rubbed his head Parvez told her that the previous evening he and Ali had gone to a restaurant. As they studied the menu, the waiter, whom Parvez knew, brought him his usual whisky and water. Parvez had been so nervous he had even prepared a question. He was going to ask Ali if he was worried about his imminent exams. But first, wanting to relax, he loosened his tie, crunched a popadom and took a long drink.

Before Parvez could speak, Ali made a face.

'Don't you know it's wrong to drink alcohol?' he said.

'He spoke to me very harshly,' Parvez told Bettina. 'I was about to castigate the boy for being insolent, but managed to control myself.'

He had explained patiently to Ali that for years he had worked more than ten hours a day, that he had few enjoyments or hobbies and never went on holiday. Surely it wasn't a crime to have a drink when he wanted one?

'But it is forbidden,' the boy said.

Parvez shrugged, 'I know.'

'And so is gambling, isn't it?'

'Yes. But surely we are only human?'

Each time Parvez took a drink, the boy winced, or made a fastidious face as an accompaniment. This made Parvez drink more quickly. The waiter, wanting to please his friend, brought another glass of whisky. Parvez knew he was getting drunk, but he couldn't stop himself. Ali had a horrible look on his face, full of disgust and censure. It was as if he hated his father.

Halfway through the meal Parvez suddenly lost his temper and threw a plate on the floor. He had felt like ripping the cloth from the table, but the waiters and other customers were staring at him. Yet he wouldn't stand for his own son telling him the difference between right and wrong. He knew he wasn't a bad man. He had a conscience. There were a few things of which he was ashamed, but on the whole he had lived a decent life.

'When have I had time to be wicked?' he asked Ali.

In a low monotonous voice the boy explained that Parvez had not, in fact, lived a good life. He had broken countless rules of the Koran.

'For instance?' Parvez demanded.

Ali hadn't needed time to think. As if he had been waiting for this moment, he asked his father if he didn't relish pork pies?

'Well. . .'

Parvez couldn't deny that he loved crispy bacon smothered with mushrooms and mustard and sandwiched between slices of fried bread. In fact he ate this for breakfast every morning.

Ali then reminded Parvez that he had ordered his own wife to cook pork sausages, saying to her, 'You're not in the village now, this is England. We have to fit in!' Parvez was so annoyed and perplexed by this attack that he called for more drink.

'The problem is this,' the boy said. He leaned across the table. For the first time that night his eyes were alive. 'You are too implicated in Western civilisation.'

Parvez burped; he thought he was going to choke.

Finsbury Park Mosque in London, which became a centre for 'jihadist' Islamic preaching associated with the extremist cleric Abu Hamza al-Mazri between 1997 and 2003

'Implicated!' he said. 'But we live here!'

'The Western materialists hate us,' Ali said. 'Papa, how can you love something which hates you?'

'What is the answer then?' Parvez said miserably. 'According to you.'

Ali addressed his father fluently, as if Parvez were a rowdy crowd that had to be quelled and convinced. The Law of Islam would rule the world; the skin of the infidel would burn off again and again; the Jews and Christians would be routed. The West was a sink of hypocrites, adulterers, homosexuals, drug takers and prostitutes.

As Ali talked, Parvez looked out of the window as if to check that they were still in London.

'My people have taken enough. If the persecution doesn't stop there will be jihad. I, and millions of others, will gladly give our lives for the cause.'

'But why, why?' Parvez said.

'For us the reward will be in paradise.'

'Paradise!'

Finally, as Parvez's eyes filled with tears, the boy urged him to mend his ways.

'How is that possible?' Parvez asked.

'Pray,' Ali said. 'Pray beside me.'

Parvez called for the bill and ushered his boy out of the restaurant as soon as he was able. He couldn't take any more. Ali sounded as if he'd swallowed someone else's voice.

On the way home the boy sat in the back of the taxi, as if he were a customer.

'What has made you like this?' Parvez asked him, afraid that somehow he was to blame for all this. 'Is there a particular event which has influenced you?'

'Living in this country.'

'But I love England,' Parvez said, watching his boy in the mirror. 'They let you do almost anything here.'

'That is the problem,' he replied.

Vocabulary

3 mac (n.): (BrE) raincoat - **14f. imminent** (adj.): coming soon - **16 popadom** (n.): large, circular, thin, crispy snack served at the beginning of a meal in an Indian restaurant - **21 to castigate** (v.): to criticize sharply - **21 insolent** (adj.): rude, disrespectful - **31 to wince** (v.): to show an expression of pain - **32 fastidious** (adj.): showing disgust - **37 censure** (n.): criticism, disapproval - **54 to relish** (v.): to enjoy - **63 perplexed** (adj.): confused and worried - **67 to be implicated in** (v.): to be involved in something bad - **68 to burp** (v.): to allow gas from the stomach to come through the mouth noisily - **90 to quell** (v.): to force to be calm - **92 infidel** (n.): non-believer, non-Muslim - **93 to rout** (v.): to defeat completely - **94 sink** (n.): (here) a swamp, a place full of dirty things - **94 hypocrite** (n.): a person who acts differently from the beliefs they claim to have - **98 persecution** (n.): being treated badly because of one's beliefs - **99 jihad** (n.): (Arabic) a holy war - **108 to usher out** (v.): to escort s.o. to the door

Explanations

91 Law of Islam: Sharia law, based on the Koran and centuries of interpretation by scholars; it sets out rules of behaviour in most spheres of life.

Awareness

1 What happened on 11 September 2001 (nine-eleven)?
2 What is the meaning of the word 'Islam'? What do you know about things Muslims are forbidden to do, and things they are expected to do?

Comprehension

3 What is Bettina's profession? What is Parvez's?
4 What aspects of Parvez's behaviour does Ali criticize?
5 Who does Ali mean when he talks about 'my people' (l. 98)?

Analysis

6 What are the effects of the use of indirect and direct speech?
7 Why has the author juxtaposed the two stories in this way?
8 In what ways does the author signal the extent to which Parvez agrees or disagrees with his son? Does Ali understand these signals?
9 What are the differences between Parvez's and Ali's conception of right and wrong?
10 Comment on the sentence: "As Ali talked, Parvez looked out of the window as if to check that they were still in London." (ll. 96f.).

Opinion

11 In what ways could this story, published in 1997, be described as prophetic?
12 Where do the sympathies of the reader lie? How are they relativized?

Projects

13 Find out about some of the different branches of Islam (e.g. Shia / Sunni / Sufi / Wahabi).
14 Watch the film *My Son the Fanatic* and compare it with this extract.
15 Read or watch other works by Hanif Kureishi about ethnic diversity in the UK, e.g. *The Buddha of Suburbia, My Beautiful Laundrette, The Black Album.*

Info

The requirements of Islam

Islam means 'submission', or the total surrender of the self to God (Allah). It originated in the seventh century with the prophet Muhammad (Mohammed), whose followers are called Muslims. Muslims follow the Sunnah (the deeds of Muhammad) and his teachings as they are written down in the Qur'an (Koran).

Most Muslims belong to two major denominations, Sunni and Shi'a. There are almost six times as many Sunni as Shi'a Muslims.

Islam claims to be the purest form of the religion of the one God, from which Jews and Christians have deviated.

Muslims believe in a life after death.

Sunni Islam has five 'pillars' of faith:

- That there is one God and that Muhammad is his prophet.
- Muslims must pray five times a day facing Mecca.
- Muslims must give money to the poor or to help spread Islam, according to their wealth.
- Muslims must fast (not eat or drink) from dawn to dusk during the month of Ramadan.
- Every able-bodied Muslim should make a pilgrimage to Mecca (Hajj) at least once in a lifetime.

In addition, Muslims should fight for their faith (Jihad), should live virtuously and avoid evil.

A system of rules and laws has grown up over time. These include rules of diet (halal food – no pork must be eaten or alcohol drunk, and animals for meat must be ritually slaughtered) and behaviour (male circumcision, eating with the right hand, using Islamic greetings, burial of the dead). Not all Muslims follow these rules strictly.

Apostasy (abandoning the Islamic religion) leads to damnation and is punishable by death.

Islam lays particular stress on sexual morality. Sex is approved of within marriage, but not outside. For this reason Islam has encouraged marriage as soon as possible after puberty. Masturbation is regarded as a sin, and sex outside marriage or homosexuality are to be severely punished, by whipping or death, although not all Islamic states apply these punishments. Marriage is a social contract, and a Muslim man may have up to four wives, provided he treats them equally, while a woman is only allowed one husband. Divorce is possible if the man says 'I divorce you' to the woman three times.

Shariah, or Islamic, courts settle disputes between people or determine penalties for misbehaviour.

14

Nadeem Aslam

"After a Murder"*

Kaukab and Shamas, immigrants from Pakistan, live in an industrial town in Northern England which has recently been the scene of a murder: Shamas' younger brother Jugnu and his girlfriend Chanda have been murdered by Chanda's brothers for living together without being married, which the brothers regarded as an attack on the family honour. Now Kaukab has cooked a meal for her sons Ujala and Charag, daughter Mah-Jabin, and her eight-year-old grandson. However, there are tensions at this family reunion, which come to the surface when Kaukab sees an article about her artist son in the magazine of a Sunday newspaper. The author, born in Pakistan in 1966, grew up in Huddersfield. – Nadeem Aslam, *Maps for Lost Lovers* (London: Faber & Faber, 2004), pp. 320 ff.

Kaukab, smiling proudly, takes the magazine and looks at Charag's photograph. *The Uncut Self-Portrait* is pictured inside too and she closes the magazine when she sees it. Charag has painted himself without any clothes standing in a pale grove of small immaculate butterflies, fruit and flower-heavy boughs, birds, hoopoes and parakeets and other insects and animals, the mist rising from a lake in the background – and he has an uncircumcised penis.

He sees the distress on her face and says, 'What I am trying to say is that it was the first act of violence done to me in the name of a religious or social system. And I wonder if anyone has the right to do it. We should all question such acts.'

'That such wickedness can be!' Kaukab says quietly. 'Why must you mock my sentiments and our religion like this?' Outside the window a large moon has appeared, its mountains and valleys a greyish black-and-white, very faint, as though it were a bad photocopy. She wishes she could fly away out of the window.

A woman in London wearing the hijab ...

'It's a *metaphor*, Mother, and, Mother, I didn't mean to offend you. Forgive me, but why does everything always have to do with you? Jugnu taught me that we should try to break away from all the bonds and ties that manipulative groups have thought up for their own advantage. Surely, mother, you see the merit of that.'

'Jugnu died because of the way he lived,' Kaukab says.

'He didn't die, Mother,' Mah Jabin says quietly. 'He was killed.'

'It is healthy to have a boy circumcised,' Shamas says, merely to come to Kaukab's aid. 'The Western doctors say it.'

'So if the doctors find out tomorrow that circumcision is unhealthy, would the Muslims stop it?' Ujala asks without looking up, face remaining tilted over his food.

'Of course not,' Kaukab says.

'I didn't think so. And, incidentally, would these Western doctors be the *same* Western doctors whose advice that first-cousins shouldn't marry each other, you lot *ignore*?'

'I fail to see what I could have possibly done to be humiliated in this manner again and again,' Kaukab says.

'I know circumcision is probably healthier,' Charag says quietly, 'and we have had our own son circumcised, but we didn't do it because of a religion. I am sorry if you are offended but I can't paint with handcuffs on.'

'I think your conduct is most regrettable. What point are you trying to make with that picture? That a religion that has given dignity to millions around the world is barbaric?'

Ujala sits back in his chair and considers Kaukab. 'Dignity? Mother, are you aware that Muslim women cannot marry a non-Muslim? Their testimony in a court of law is worth half that of a man. Non-Muslims living in Muslim countries have inferior status under Islamic law: they may not testify against a Muslim. Non-believers are to be killed: of the seventeen great sins in Islam, unbelief is the greatest, worse than murder, theft, adultery. In Saudi Arabia, following a saying of Muhammad that "Two religions cannot exist in Arabia", non-Muslims are forbidden to practise their religion, build churches, possess Bibles.' His voice has risen a little and the eight-year-old looks furiously at him, and, chest out, says, 'Stop shouting, you!' Ujala reaches across the table and ruffles his hair, 'Sorry'; his fingertips briefly tickled by the penny-size area at the top of his head which always resists flattening, sticking up like the crest of a thistle.

'How do you know all this all of a sudden?' Kaukab, who was on her way out, turns around and asks Ujala.

'I've read the Koran, in English, unlike you who just chant it in Arabic without knowing what the words mean, hour after hour, day in day out, like chewing gum for the brain.'

Kaukab says, 'What I don't understand is why when you all spend your time talking about women's rights, don't you ever think about *me*. What about *my* rights, *my* feelings? Am *I* not a woman, am I a eunuch?'

Ujala continues, 'A religion that has given dignity to millions around the world? Amputations, stoning to death, flogging – not barbaric?'

'These punishments are of divine origin and cannot be judged by human criteria.'

He looks at her. 'If I changed my religion in a country like Pakistan what would happen to me, Mother?'

'Please let's continue with our meal,' Shamas says, not wishing to be reminded too much of his father's death.

... and another wearing the niqab (see p. 47)

Vocabulary

5 grove (n.): small group of trees – **5 immaculate** (adj.): perfect and pure – **6 bough** (n.): literary word for branch – **7 hoopoe** (n.): a crested bird, common in India and occasionally seen in Britain – **7 parakeet** (n.): small brightly-coloured bird, common in India – **9 uncircumcised** (adj.): with the skin at the end of the penis not cut off – **15 wickedness** (n.): behaving in a way that is morally wrong – **32f. manipulative** (adj.): clever at controlling or deceiving people to get what they want – **48 tilted** (adj.): held at an angle – **50 incidentally** (adv.): by the way – **52 first-cousins** (n.): children of brothers or sisters – **53 to ignore** (v.): to pay no attention to – **55 to humiliate** (v.): to try to make s.o. feel ashamed or stupid - **60 offended** (adj.): upset and angry - **61 conduct** (n.): behaviour - **63 dignity** (n.): a sense of value and importance - **67 testimony** (n.): a formal statement to say s.th. is true - **70 to testify** (v.): to give testimony - **92 eunuch** (n.): /ˈjuːnək/ s.o. (usually a man) whose sex organs have been removed - **100 criteria** (pl. n.): standards used to judge s.th.

Explanations

86 chant it in Arabic: the Koran is quoted, sung and studied in Arabic, the language in which it was written, even in countries where no Arabic is spoken - **94 amputations:** Sharia law includes punishments like cutting off hands for theft.

Awareness

1 Which countries in the world are Islamic or have important Muslim communities?

Comprehension

2 Why is Kaukab so offended by Charag's painting?
3 List the things which Ujala criticizes about the practice of Islam in some societies.

Analysis

4 "It's a *metaphor*, Mother" (l. 21). What does Charag mean?
5 Why do Kaukab, Shamas and the little boy all want the discussion to be ended? Analyse their reasons.
6 Try to characterize the members of the family from this discussion.
7 Analyse the replies given by Kaukab and Shamas to Ujala's points.
8 Explain the phrase "the bonds and ties that manipulative groups have thought up for their own advantage" (ll. 31 ff.).
9 Comment on the simile "like chewing gum for the brain" (ll. 87f.).

Opinion

10 Many Muslim women say, like Kaukab, that they are grateful for the rules of Islam. What might their reasons be?
11 "I can't paint with handcuffs on." (l. 60) Should an artist/writer be free to express anything at all? (Compare the affairs of the 'Danish Mohammed cartoons' in 2005 and Salman Rushdie's 'Satanic Verses'.)
12 Compare the great world religions. If a religion claims to be the one true religion, how can it tolerate others?

Projects

13 Compare the themes used in this extract with similar themes dealt with in the film *East is East.*
14 Jugnu and his lover were murdered in a so-called 'honour killing'. Use the Internet or other sources to find out more about such killings and how, why and where they happen.
15 The text points out that many Muslims are taught the Koran in a foreign language. Compare the teaching of the Christian religion over much of its history.

Info

Islamic Dress

According to most Islamic scholars, Muslims are supposed to conform to standards of 'hijab', a word originally meaning modesty, privacy and morality. There is no agreement about what clothes exactly should be worn, either by men or women.
Generally, women are expected to cover every part of their body except the face and hands. This usually means wearing long dresses or cloaks (the chador) with a covering over the head. This is usually called the 'hijab'. Some Muslim women also cover their faces, leaving just a slit for the eyes. This is called the 'niqab'. The 'burqa', worn in Afghanistan, is a garment which covers the whole head and body, leaving only a woven grille in front of the eyes to allow the wearer to see.
Men should wear loose-fitting modest clothing and should cover their heads, particularly during prayer. Some men avoid western-style clothes (T-shirt and jeans, or suits and ties) as a political statement.
The use of dress to make political points has meant that the Islamic dress code has become controversial in many countries.

15

Abdulrazak Gurnah

"An Asylum-Seeker"*

Abdulrazak Gurnah was born in 1948 on the island of Zanzibar, which later became part of Tanzania. He left to study in the UK in 1968, and is now Professor of Literature at the University of Kent and the author of several novels and short stories. Following independence in Tanzania, as in many former British colonies in Africa, authoritarian governments and political unrest, or civil wars, have led to refugees arriving in the UK from all over the continent. As a reaction to mounting opposition within Britain to immigration of this sort, successive governments have made it increasingly difficult to obtain asylum, and asylum-seekers are regularly kept in detention while their cases are considered. In Gurnah's novel *By the Sea*, the narrator's silence on arrival as an asylum-seeker in the UK from Tanzania will eventually lead to the telling of his story about the man whose name he has borrowed as an alias. – Abdulrazak Gurnah, *By the Sea* (London: Bloomsbury, 2001), pp. 41–44

A 16th century Persian miniature illustrating the Miraj

Her name is Rachel. She told me that the first day I met her when she came to visit me at the detention centre. 'I'm a legal adviser with the refugee organisation that has taken on your case. My name is Rachel Howard,' she said, smiling, offering her hand, pleased to meet you.

And my name is Rajab Shaaban. It is not my real name, but a name I borrowed for the occasion of this life-saving trip. It belonged to someone I knew for many years. Shaaban is also the name of the eighth month of the year, the month of division, when the destinies of the coming year are fixed and the sins of the truly penitent are absolved. It precedes the month of Ramadhan, the month of the great heat, the month of fasting. Rajab is the month which precedes both, the seventh month, the revered month. It was during Rajab that the night of the Miraj occurred, when the Prophet was taken through the seven heavens to the Presence of God. How we loved that story when we were young. On the night of the 27th of Rajab, the Prophet was sleeping when the Angel Jibreel woke him and made him mount the winged beast Burakh, who took him through the sky to al-Quds, Jerusalem. There, in the ruins of the Temple Mount, he prayed with Abraham, Moses and Jesus and then ascended in their company to the Lote Tree of the Uttermost Limit, sidrat almuntaha, which was the nearest that any being could approach the Almighty. The Prophet received God's injunction that Muslims were to pray fifty times in a day. On his way back, Moses advised him to return and haggle. He had been in the business a lot longer than the Prophet, and guessed that God would probably come down a bit. The Almighty came down to five times a day. In the telling of the story, a great sigh would issue from the congregation at this point. Imagine praying fifty times every single day. Then the Prophet returned to al-Quds and mounted the beast Burakh again, who flew him back to Makka before morning. There he had to face the inevitable carping and doubting from the benighted jahals of that town, but to the believers the miracle of the Miraj is an event of joyous celebration. Rajab preceded Shaaban which preceded Ramadhan, three holy months. Though God had only commanded that we fast during Ramadhan, the pious fasted throughout the three months. That was the holy joke my name-sake's parents played on him, calling him Rajab when his father's name was Shaaban, like calling him July when his father's name was August, and no doubt they had a good chuckle but he paid for it, the name. As I would have done, if my parents had really given me that name.

I didn't say any of this to Rachel Howard when she came to see me at the detention centre. I didn't say anything. To call it a detention centre is to be melodramatic. There were no locked gates or armed guards, not even a uniform in sight. It was an encampment in the countryside, which was run by a private company. There were three large structures that looked like sheds or warehouses, where they gave us a place to sleep and fed us. It was cold. The wind howled and wailed outside, gusting at times as if it would lift the whole building and hurl it away. I felt as if the blood in my veins had stopped flowing, had turned into sharp-edged crystals which bit into my inner flesh. When I stopped moving my limbs went numb. We slept in two of the buildings, twelve in one and ten in the other, our sleeping spaces partitioned with boards but without doors. Each building had a toilet and a shower, and a separate tap labelled 'Drinking Water.' I wondered about that, and whether it meant I should use the shower with circumspection, whether the water was safe. We ate in the third building, food delivered to us in a van in large square metal containers. It was served to us by a middle-aged Englishman of crumpled and gloomy appearance, not a specimen I had met yet in my travels at that point, but which I have seen in large numbers since. In fact many of the people I met in those early months surprised me in appearance. They seemed so unlike the straight-backed, unsmiling variety I remembered from years ago. Our Englishman was called Harold, and he served our food as well as cleaned the showers and the toilets in his own fashion. [...]

There were twenty-two men in the camp. The twelve in our building were four Algerians, three Ethiopians, two Iranian brothers just out of their teens, who clung to each other and whispered and sobbed in the night before they fell asleep in the same bed, a Sudanese and an Angolan, who was the dynamo and live-wire of our establishment, bursting with advice, with jokes, with politics, with deals, with the righteousness of Unita's cause in the war. No Nigerians here, the Angolan told us. Too many of them in detention and they're too much trouble, so they have to be kept under lock and key in an old castle in the frozen north, away from human habitation. Too many of them in the world altogether. His name was Alfonso, and he had a deep and unrelenting antipathy to Nigerians, which he did not explain but which illuminated every day of his life, it seemed. He had been in the camp, the barracks as he preferred to call it, for several weeks. He refused to be moved, saying he needed the seclusion and the rural air to finish the book he was writing. If he went and mingled with the English in the streets and spent all his evenings in their pubs watching football on TV, he would lose the edge of his recollections and there would be no point to anything he had done. He liked it there in the barracks among his rootless brethren, thank you. The detainees in the other building were all from south Asia, from India and Sri Lanka, and perhaps people of Indian origin from elsewhere. I don't know. They conducted their affairs separately from us, sat together as a group during meals, and seemed to have a language with which to speak to one another which was not comprehensible to the rest of us.

It was to the small building, which contained a dispensary, an office and some kind of consulting-room, that I was summoned to meet Rachel Howard.

Vocabulary

7 detention centre (n.): a place to hold people, like a prison - **25 penitent** (adj.): feeling sorry for having sinned, and determined not to do it again - **25f. to absolve** (v.): to forgive - **26 to precede** (v.): to come before - **28f. revered** (adj.): treated with religious respect - **41 injunction** (n.): order, instruction - **43 to haggle** (v.): to bargain, argue about how much s.th. should be - **47 congregation** (n.): a group of people gathered together, usually for a religious service - **52 carping** (n.): complaining and criticism - **52 benighted** (adj.): having no understanding - **52 jahal** (n.): Arabic word for ignoramus (s.o. who knows nothing) - **53 miracle** (n.): s.th. normally impossible done by God - **27 to fast** (v.): to go without food at some times - **58 name-sake** (n.): s.o. with the same name - **61 chuckle** (n.): laugh - **66f. to be melodramatic** (v.): to exaggerate - **77 numb** (adj.): without feeling - **83 with circumspection** (adv.): carefully, cautiously - **86 crumpled** (adj.): with folds or lines - **86 gloomy** (adj.): depressed, pessimistic - **87 specimen** (n.): an example of a type of person - **98 to sob** (v.): to cry noisily - **100 dynamo** (n.): s.o. who does things with energy - **100 live wire** (n.): a very lively person - **109 antipathy** (n.): strong dislike - **111 barracks** (pl. n.): buildings where soldiers live - **113 seclusion** (n.): being alone - **123 to conduct their affairs** (v.): to do what they did - **127f. dispensary** (n.): place where medicines are given out - **128 consulting-room** (n.): place where a doctor sees a patient - **129 to summon** (v.): to order s.o. to come

Explanations

34 Jibreel: the Arabic name for Gabriel - **36f. ruins of the Temple Mount:** The Jewish Temple built by Solomon and Herod was demolished by the Romans in 70AD. The Dome of the Rock and al-Aqsa Mosque were built on the site. - **38 Lote Tree:** Not a physical tree, it is a metaphor for the limits of human understanding - **50 Makka:** alternative spelling of Mecca - **102 Unita:** Founded in 1966, the Unita party fought for the independence of Angola from the Portuguese, and later in a civil war against the Russian-backed MPLA government. The war ended with the death of Unita's leader, Jonas Savimbi, in 2002.

Awareness

1 Find out about the history and culture of Zanzibar and Tanganyika.

Comprehension

2 Explain what the reader learns about the significance of the names the narrator has adopted for Muslims.
3 What does the story reveal about the relationship between the 'three great monotheistic religions'?
4 Why does Rachel Howard come to see the narrator?
5 Summarize the conditions under which detainees are held, and who is responsible for them.

Analysis

6 "I didn't say any of this to Rachel Howard" (l. 64). What is the effect of not knowing the meaning of the names?
7 Why does Alfonso prefer to stay in the detention centre? How does his reason relate to the narrator's story?
8 Why is the narrator surprised by Harold?
9 Analyse the language in which the story of the Miraj is told. What effect does it have?

Opinion

10 Why are asylum-seekers kept in detention and not allowed to work?
11 What are the arguments for and against giving asylum to refugees?

Projects

12 Find out about the obligations the UK and other nations have towards refugees.
13 Explain why the different nationalities at the centre might have come to Britain. Find out about the political situations in the countries mentioned.

16

"Fuelling Resentment"*

Some people in the UK feel they are being 'swamped' by immigrants and asylum-seekers. Some newspapers, particularly tabloid papers like the *Daily Mail*, the *Express* and the *Sun*, have often run stories about 'bogus' asylum seekers, suggesting that the country is full of foreign criminals and scroungers living off British taxpayers. Are they reflecting public anger about abuses and faults in the system, or are they contributing to negative and misleading stereotypes? - THE SUN , Friday, 9 August 2002, p.17

MIGRANTS TAKE US TO THE CLEANERS

Asylum rejects get free laundry at luxury 'hotel'

by KATHRYN LISTER

HUNDREDS of illegal immigrants are taking UK taxpayers to the cleaners while they wait to be deported.

Refugees are being pampered in hotel-class accommodation and even have a free next-day laundry service.

Their luxury lifestyle includes use of a gym, pool tables, colour TVs in every room and a personal paging service for incoming phone calls.

Teams of cleaners and chefs are shuttled in each day to look after the illegals whose applications for asylum have been rejected.

Homely

They are kept in comfort thanks to taxpayers shelling out £1.3million to refurbish a disused young offenders' institute at Dover, Kent, with top-class leisure facilities.

The centre has new beds and a modernized surgery with daily visits from GPs. The old cells have even been painted in subtle shades of pink and green to make them feel more homely.

About 200 asylum seekers, at various stages of deportation, are being treated to the new facilities. Once they leave Britain they are quickly replaced by more rejected refugees.

But the centre – which opened in April and is run by the Prison Service – has caused outrage among local residents.

Insurance clerk Theresa Hewitt, 32, fumed: "The refugee crisis is getting worse, but this takes the biscuit.

"Most of us are hard-working taxpayers yet these people live in luxury compared to us. I wish I could afford to go to a gym and have a personal laundry service and cleaner. Enjoying a lifestyle like this will only make these people more determined to get back to Britain."

Chris Ryan, 48, said: "Some of us have to scrape a living while refugees watch telly as their laundry's done or have a game of pool while their dinner's cooked for them."

All mod cons... illegal immigrants enjoy pampering at special centre

The ex-lifeboat rescue worker added: "When illegal immigrants get this five-star treatment it's no wonder they are keen to come here.

"They must feel like there's a pot of gold waiting for them. It's outrageous how much this crisis is costing our country."

Tory councillor Alan Watkins said: "Many hard-working low-income families, pensioners and disabled folk would love to enjoy these kind of facilities but can't afford them. It's a real scandal."

Comfort

Last night a Home Office spokesman said: "These people have not committed any crimes and deserve to be treated with dignity and respect.

"They are not staying in luxury accommodation but there is some level of comfort.

"It would be inhumane to keep them locked up with nothing to do for 24 hours a day.

"They will all eventually be removed from the UK, but during that time their needs are very different to those of prisoners."

Vocabulary

caption: all mod cons: with every comfort (from estate agents' brochures: all modern conveniences) - **caption: pampering** (n.): being looked after very well - **headline: reject** (n.): s.o. not accepted - **headline: laundry** (n.): clothes cleaning service - **2 to deport** (v.): to remove from the country - **5 pool** (n.): game of billiards - **6 paging** (n.): informing s.o. if they are wanted - **8 to shuttle** (v.): to move people from one place to another (e.g. by bus) - **9 illegal** (n.): (infml.) illegal immigrant - **12 to shell out** (v.): (infml.): to pay - **13 to refurbish** (v.): to repair and redecorate - **13f. young offenders' institute** (n.): prison for young people - **15 surgery** (n.): (BrE) a place where a doctor examines and gives treatment - **16 GP** (n.): general practitioner, a medical doctor who deals with all kinds of problems - **24 outrage** (n.): great anger - **25 to fume** (v.): to say angrily - **26 to take the biscuit** (v.): (infml.) to be the worst thing - **29 gym** (n.): fitness centre - **32 to scrape a living** (v.): to work hard for only just enough money - **42 pensioner** (n.): someone who is retired and is paid a pension - **51 inhumane** (adj.): extremely cruel and causing suffering - **53 eventually** (adv.): in the end

Explanations

14 Dover, Kent: Dover, and the south-eastern county of Kent, have a large number of asylum seekers, because they are nearest to the harbour where many asylum seekers arrive. - **41 Tory councillor:** a member of a local council for the Conservative party - **46 Home Office:** the government department for internal affairs, which is responsible for administering the asylum system.

Awareness

1 Why do people leave their homes and travel to places like the UK, which are hard to enter?

Comprehension

2 What sort of building was/is the asylum centre?
3 What aspects of the way the centre is run interest the reporter?
4 What points are made by the Home Office spokesman?

Analysis

5 Analyse the structure of the article.
6 Comment on the headlines and caption and their use of language. Say something about the words chosen for the cross-heads as well.
7 Comment on the sort of ordinary people the reporter has chosen to interview. What appears to be her intention?
8 Try to deduce from the text whether the people interviewed are reacting to the asylum centre, or to the story in the newspaper about it.
9 Note where words have been used in emotive ways in the article.
10 What is the effect of including the Home Office spokesman's comments at the end of the article?

Opinion

11 The last sentence of the introduction before the article poses a question. What do your findings in Task 8 indicate is the answer?
12 What do articles like these suggest about the newspapers that print them, and their readers?
13 Why do governments pay for asylum-seekers?
14 Can one say that someone who has come to Western Europe because he cannot feed his family is a 'bogus' asylum-seeker?

Creative Writing

15 Find out from the internet where refugees come from and what conditions are like there. Imagine you are seeking asylum. Write part of your application and explain why you have come to Britain.

Info

The British Press: the 'tabloids' and the 'serious' papers

Most daily newspapers in the UK are national dailies, published in London and distributed around the country. British newspapers can be divided into three groups:

- **Quality** papers, which used to be broadsheet size but now vary from tabloid to broadsheet, concentrate on national and international news, politics, business, arts and social issues.
- **Popular** papers, which are all tabloid size, concentrate on domestic news, personal interest, fashion and lifestyle, and the private lives of celebrities.
- **Sensational** papers, also tabloid size, concentrate on domestic news, shocking or amusing stories, scandals involving famous people, TV, film and music stars.

Because the popular and sensational papers used to be the only ones of tabloid size, they were called 'the tabloids', and this name is still used for them. The sensational tabloids are also called 'red tops' because their names are printed in red.

Tabloids have strip cartoons, games and horoscopes.
All the newspapers have sports sections, weather and TV schedules.
All the newspapers separate news stories from comment articles.

Tabloid news stories have banner headlines, large pictures, very short paragraphs. They often use alliterations, puns, allusions and nicknames in headlines, and colloquial register in the articles. Comment articles are short and more like slogans, giving only one opinion.

Serious papers have smaller headlines and slightly longer paragraphs. They use a more formal register. Comment articles have a distinct line of argument, usually discussing two possible views, but finally choosing one opinion. Serious papers are beginning to adopt some of the characteristics of the tabloids, like using puns in headlines.

All news stories tend to be structured in a similar way:
1) headline (to arouse the reader's interest)
2) summary of news point (main facts)
3) news story in detail
4) background of news story
5) other implications, results, etc. (arousing interest in reading back)

Newspapers often have a particular political or social agenda, depending on the political opinions of their owners, readers or editors. In reading articles from particular papers, one needs to be aware of these agendas.

17

Marina Lewycka

"Dreams"*

After the EU enlargement of 2004, citizens of the new member states were allowed to enter the UK freely to live and work. Of the other EU states only Sweden and Ireland gave the same rights. As a result, Britain experienced its biggest post-war influx of immigrants from Poland, the Czech republic and the Baltic states (estimated at more than 750,000 in the following three years), completely changing the character of the ethnic mix in the UK. Marina Lewycka, born to Ukrainian parents in a refugee camp in Germany in 1946, lives and works in Sheffield. *Two Caravans*, her second novel, deals with the world of the new immigrants to the UK. In this extract, Tomasz, from Poland, has taken work on a chicken farm in Kent, putting thousands of chickens in cages to prepare them for transportation to the slaughterhouse. Neil, the son of the foreman, has been showing him how to do it.
– Marina Lewycka, *Two Caravans* (London: Penguin Fig Tree, 2007), pp. 204 ff.

Outside in the sunshine, they take deep gulps of air and splash themselves with water from a tap at the side of the barn. Then they slump in a line on the ground along the wall. Neil takes out his half-cigarette and has a few puffs, coughing away with a determined look on his face.

'Getting there, getting there,' he says.

The Portuguese, or the Brazilians, light up cigarettes too. They have unzipped their overalls, and Tomasz can see that they are wearing nothing but underpants underneath. In fact one of them doesn't even seem to be

Intensive poultry farming

wearing underpants. That is sensible, he thinks. Then he thinks about the too-tight-in-the-crotch overall that he is wearing. Who wore it before? He turns to the young man who is sitting next to him. He is a bit shorter than Neil, and probably about the same age, with curly hair and beautiful teeth.

'Portuguese?'

'Yes,' says the young man.

'Brazilian?'

'Yes.'

Tomasz points at himself.

'Polish. Poland.'

'Ah!' The young man beams. 'Gregor Lato.'

'Pele,' says Tomasz. They shake hands.

'You like football?'

'Of course,' says Tomasz, for the sake of friendship, even though it is not strictly true, as he finds all sport tedious, but if anything would prefer to watch Juvenia Krakow play rugby. It is one of those little areas of dissent he has carved out for himself, like drinking wine instead of beer and listening to foreign music.

'Later we play.' The young man's teeth flash in a smile.

'Later we play bagpipe.' The other man sitting next to him has a mad glint in his eye.

'Scottish?' Tomasz asks.

He winks at Tomasz. 'Scottish.'

As they are finishing their cigarettes a huge lorry trundles up, and the four men jump to their feet and go across to talk to the driver, who also seems to be Portuguese. Or Brazilian.

'They are from Portugal or Brazil?' Tomasz asks Neil.

'Yeah. One or the other. Some are Portugeezers pretending to be Brazils. Some are Brazils pretending to be Portugeezers.'

'They pretend to be Brazil?'

'Yeah, mad, innit? Yer see Brazils are illegal, so they get in by saying they're Portugeezers. But the Portugeezers are legal now, wiv that Europe like marketing fing, and some of 'em've been making trouble, so nobody wants to take 'em on any more. That's what me dad says.'

'They making trouble?'

'Yeah, trade unions. Minimum wage. Elf and safety. Brazils don't cause trouble, see, 'cause they're illegal. So if the Portugeezers want a job, they have to pretend to be Brazillers – Portugeezers pretending to be Brazillers pretending to be Portugeezers. Mad, innit? [...]

'What is minimum wage in UK?'

'I dunno. Not much. Do you have that where you come from? Poland?'

'We have one very famous trade union. Is name Solidarnosc. You know it?'

'Sounds like something you could get yer teeth into. Solid-er nosh. Heh heh. Geddit? Yeah, I reckon I'm going to Brazil.' He throws in this bit of information so casually that Tomasz, who is still thinking about trade unions, almost misses it. He looks at the lad with renewed interest.

'So you make voyage of discovery?'

He had been like that at Neil's age, always looking for a way out. Of course, when he was seventeen, that had been in communist times, and the only journeys to be made were the inward ones. He remembers how one of his friends had got hold of a pirated tape of Bob Dylan and they had sat, four of them, in his father's car locked inside the garage, the windows misted up with their spellbound breath, listening to the music as though it was the chimes of freedom. In every life there is a moment when you can break free of taken-for-granted situations and strike out in a different direction. That evening had been a turning point in his life. He had taught himself English in order to understand the words, and a few months later he bought a second-hand guitar from a Czech gipsy who happened to be passing through Zdroj. And he made himself a promise: one day he would come to the West.

'Voyage of discovery? Heh heh. I like that,' said Neil. 'One day, when I save up enough, I'm going to Brazil. It's my dream. Everybody's got to have a dream. That's why I'm learnin' to smoke.' He looks across at the four Portuguese-Brazilians, who have zipped up their overalls and are making their way back to the barn. 'Maybe their dream was coming to England. Come to England and work up to yer ankles in chicken shit. Funny dream, eh?'

Vocabulary

1 gulp (n.): large amount of air breathed in quickly – **3 to slump** (v.): to sit down heavily because one is tired – **4 puff** (n.): action of taking smoke from a cigarette – **12 crotch** (n.): part of the body between the tops of the legs – **28 tedious** (adj.): boring – **30 dissent** (n.): refusal to share an accepted opinion – **39 to trundle** (v.): to move slowly and heavily on wheels – **48 innit?:** (isn't it?) all-purpose question tag, commonly used by young people – **61 dunno:** don't know – **66 nosh** (n.): (BrE infml.) food – **76 pirated** (adj.): illegally obtained or copied – **79 spellbound** (adj.): fascinated – **80 chime** (n.): ringing of a bell – **86 gipsy** (n.): (also Gypsy) member of a group of nomadic people, originally from India, also called Romanies

Explanations

23f. Gregor Lato, Pele: famous footballers for Poland and Brazil – **34 play bagpipe:** He means a 'game' of squeezing a chicken to spray excrement – **44f. Portugeezers, Brazils:** Neil's names for Portuguese and Brazilians involve making foreign words sound like English ones, in this case 'geezer' (infml. for 'man') and brazil nut – **49f. Portugeezers are legal now:** After Portugal joined the EU in 1986 Portuguese workers were free to take jobs in the UK – **50 Europe like marketing fing:** Originally known in Britain as the 'Common Market', the European Union remains a controversial political idea in the UK. – **55 Elf and safety:** Trade unions insist that employers observe health and safety regulations. – **63f. Solidarnosc:** Polish word for 'solidarity'; the union, under Lech Walesa, played a large part in undermining the communist regime in Poland in the 1970s and 1980s. – **74 in communist times:** Under communist control in Eastern Europe (1945–89), it was impossible for most people to travel outside the Soviet bloc, and anything the authorities considered subversive was banned. – **76f. Bob Dylan:** the most important singer-songwriter to emerge from the 1960s musical revolution – **87 Zdroj:** The name of Tomasz's hometown in Poland means 'spring'; there are several towns in Southern Poland with this name.

Awareness

1 What do you know about agricultural work and who does it?

Comprehension

2 Why is Neil exceptional on this farm?
3 Explain in your own words why it is unclear whether the other workers are Brazilian or Portuguese.
4 What is meant by 'inward' journeys (l. 75)?
5 What made Tomasz want to come to England?

Analysis

6 What can be deduced about the work the men have been doing?
7 Determine the narrative perspective in this extract.
8 Try to characterise Tomasz, Neil and the Portuguese/Brazilians, paying attention to their use of English.
9 Comment on Neil's reply when he is asked if he knows Solidarnosc.

Opinion

10 Explain the ironies involved in the idea of a 'dream'. Does the text suggest an alternative way of looking at the idea?
11 Would you like to live and work in another EU country? If so, which, and why?

Projects

12 Find out about industrial farming techniques and the different conditions under which animals are kept. Use the results to have a debate about human needs and animal rights.
13 Find out about the career of Bob Dylan and look closely at some of his songs (e.g. 'Blowing in the Wind', 'The Times They Are A-Changing', 'One Too Many Mornings', 'Chimes of Freedom', 'It's All-right, Ma', 'Visions of Johanna', 'Tangled Up In Blue', 'Knocking on Heaven's Door', 'Union Sundown', 'Not Dark Yet', 'Nettie Moore').

Internet Projects

14 Tomasz bought his guitar from a Gypsy. Use the internet to find out about Romany Gypsies and their presence in the UK.
15 Imagine you are working in the UK. Make up an internet blog to describe your experiences of ethnic diversity.

18

Geoffrey Alderman

"Immigration and Resentment"*

100 years ago, when numerous Jewish immigrants entered Britain, the state offered little or no assistance. Do today's immigrants find it easier to start a new life in the UK, or does help from the welfare state merely cause resentment? Professor Geoffrey Alderman (b. 1944) is a historian and journalist who contributes to *The Guardian* and *The Jewish Chronicle*. On the website where this article from the paper appeared, readers have an opportunity of making their own contributions to the discussion. - *The Guardian*, 19 November 2007

Traditionally dressed Yiddish-speaking Jews enjoy a family day out at the London Zoo

Immigration and the treatment of immigrants are likely to feature prominently in political and public discourse in this country between now and the next general election. There is absolutely no reason why this should not be so. Britain has always attracted immigrants – the only truly indigenous "English" are the Celts, pushed by the Romans out of England and into what are now Wales and the west country. After the Romans came the Anglo-Saxons, and after them the Normans, and later still the Huguenots and the Irish, and assorted Germans and Italians. Then – 150 years ago – came the Russians and the Romanians and the Poles, many though not all of whom were Jewish. After 1945, there were large influxes of people of African descent, and later from Asia. More recently, there has been a further influx from Poland and other eastern European countries.

All these immigrant groups, with the exception of the Anglo-Saxons and the Normans (who came as conquerors) suffered discrimination, and there is a remarkable similarity with respect to the accusations that were made about them. The Jews were accused of robbing true Britons of their daily bread by agreeing to work longer hours for lower wages. The Jews, it was said, caused housing shortages and brought diseases into this country. But the most telling accusation made against the Jews was that they were "a people apart." When the Jews moved into a neighbourhood (the accusation ran), its "English" (or "Scottish," or "Welsh") character was compromised. Churches became synagogues. Jewish scents replaced "English" (or "Scottish," or "Welsh") fragrances.

Some of these accusations were true: Jewish migrants did indeed spread tuberculosis. Others were false: there were inner-city housing crises in Glasgow, Manchester, Leeds and London well before the Jews (or, to be more exact, poor Jews) arrived. But who can seriously argue that the Jews have not, by their endeavours, immeasurably enriched the economic, social and cultural life of the UK? And, for all the genuine fears about the Jewish influx a hundred years ago, when all is said and done there are at most only around 300,000 of us here now. Britain has done well by its Jews. Its Jews have done well by Britain.

Perhaps for these reasons, British Jews are unwilling to enter the current debate about immigration. In fact, we Jews are in the position of being able to offer a unique perspective, and to make a unique contribution to the debate. [...]

The basic issue surrounding immigrants in Britain today is not their colour or their creed. It is their impact, unchecked, on our social infrastructure. For my ancestors who came to these shores this was much less of an issue. There was no welfare state to speak of, only charity. The tombstones of my maternal great-grandfather at Edmonton and of my wife's maternal grandfather at Streatham actually list the Jewish friendly societies (self-help in action) to which they belonged. From the state they asked for and received nothing.

What causes so much disquiet, prejudice and anger is the sight of newly-arrived immigrants receiving taxpayers' money and benefits in kind when they have yet to make any tax contribution themselves. If it was made clear to would-be immigrants that, upon arrival, they will receive nothing, or next-to-nothing, from the state, many would think much harder about coming here, and those that do would be under no illusion as to the state's expectations of them.

We do need an honest, grown-up debate about immigration. As part of that debate we should ask whether the structure of British society 100 years ago, with all its admitted faults and inequalities, was nonetheless actually more conducive to the reception and settlement of immigrants in this country.

Vocabulary

2 to feature prominently (v.): to play an important role – **2 public discourse** (n.): serious written or spoken discussions, for instance in the media – **6 indigenous** (adj.): native, having been there from the beginning – **13 influx** (n.): large numbers coming in – **20 with respect to** (prep.): concerning – **29 scent** (n.): pleasant smell, fragrance – **36 endeavours** (n.): efforts, hard work – **39 when all is said and done:** in spite of that – **41 to do well by** (v.): to help, treat well – **46 perspective** (n.): way of seeing s.th. – **49 creed** (n.): belief, religion – **53 maternal** (adj.): on the mother's side of the family – **60 benefits in kind** (n.): things, rather than money, given by the government – **60f. have yet to make:** have not yet made – **62 would-be immigrants** (n.): people who want to immigrate – **65 to be under no illusion as to:** understand very clearly, not see too positively – **70 an admitted fault** (n.): something we now agree was wrong – **71 conducive to** (adj.): with the right conditions for

Explanations

6 Celts: people who lived in Britain before the Romans came. They spoke a language that was the ancestor of Welsh – **7 Romans:** Britain was conquered by the Romans in 43 AD. Latin was the official language. The Romans stayed until about 410 AD. – **8f. Anglo-Saxons:** People from the coastal areas of Germany. They conquered what is now England (Angle-land). They spoke an old form of German. – **9 Normans:** People of mixed Norwegian and French descent; they conquered England in 1066 under William the Conqueror. They spoke old French. – **10 Huguenots:** French Protestants who fled from religious persecution in the 16th century. – **10 Irish:** Irish people came to work in Britain from the 18th until the 20th century to escape from poverty and starvation. – **10f. Germans and Italians:** Political and economic refugees came from Germany and Italy in the mid-19th century. – **11f. Russians, Romanians, Poles:** Mostly Jews, but also Romany Gypsies, escaped from pogroms in Eastern Europe in the late 19th century. – **14 people of African descent:** Africans and people from the Caribbean. – **14 Asia:** the Indian subcontinent and China. – **22 daily bread:** the means of making a living (the phrase is an allusion to the Lord's Prayer) – **55f. friendly societies:** clubs, often organized in lodges, which provided money for members in difficulty. The members paid into the club if they were doing well. Many friendly societies still exist.

Awareness

1 Find out about the population make-up of the UK and how it was influenced by migration.
2 What do you know about Jewish immigration to Britain? Where did Jews come from? What sort of work did they do? Where did they live? What language did they speak?

Comprehension

3 According to the author, what accusations did people make against Jewish immigrants? Which were true and which were false?
4 What differences does the author perceive between Jewish immigrants and immigrants today?
5 Explain the difference between 'the welfare state' and 'charity'.

Analysis

6 Outline the structure of the author's argument.
7 What are the meanings of the phrases: "a people apart" (l. 26), "their impact, unchecked, on our social infrastructure" (ll. 49f.) and "an honest, grown-up debate" (l. 67); what are their implications?
8 Comment on the sentences: "Britain has done well by its Jews. Its Jews have done well by Britain." (ll. 41f.) to explain the relationship between form and content.
9 Analyse and comment on the four contributions taken from the thread following this article on the internet (below). What can be said about the writers and their comments (including their use of English)?

Opinion

10 What can be seen as ironic about the points Alderman makes?
11 Write a comment of your own to add to this thread in the forum (either about the original article or one of the comments).
12 What can be learnt about British Jews from the statements on p. 59? What might lead them to have a conflict of identity / loyalties?

Project

13 Find out about the Jewish religion and Jewish culture in the UK.

Internet Project

14 Try to make profiles of prominent Jews in the UK and the fields they are well known in.

Words and phrases for contributors to internet forums / discussion threads:

have your say
discussion forum / board
login name / alias
password
thread
comment / post
registered user
poster
administrator
report this comment
recommend this comment

Discussion thread from *Guardian Unlimited* website:

dissidentjunk:
I think Alderman is right.

When my grandfather came to the UK in the late 40s, there was a bit of racism but, aside from that, people did accept him into their wholly white working-class English community and didn't grumble about his presence. Today, he thinks that this is because there were no handouts at the time. He had to work; otherwise, him and his family would have nowhere to live and they would starve. Working also meant he made English friends, and socialised with English people as well as other members of his community. And as his migrant community was small in the area, there was no visible stress on the existing infrastructure.

Now he grumbles about the new immigrants, some of whom he shares his original nationality and ethnic origin, sponging off the state and getting houses and benefits when he only has a little pension, and has never asked for anything, and his grandaughter can't afford a house, and there's no good jobs for young people ... and so on.

PinkTaco:
Migration should always come at the risk and cost of the immigrant. Government has no role in supporting the private choices of the individual, especially when they are neither British subjects nor taxpayers.

Fenn:
Why cant we have a strict border control, the gov have no idea how many illegals there are. I think due to the fact that majority of middle England fund the large social underclass, as the rich offshore bank / tax avoid etc.

So I think we assume we will be funding these illegals too, why cant we have a forced count of the entire population, shut the gates and re-evaluate. Kick the non-UK criminals & illegals out, then only allow immigration for skilled workers who have jobs to go to, and make them work for at least 2 years before they can claim benifits, healthcare can be free if their working.

Yesterday:
Does the writer mean 'immigrants' or asylum seekers? It would be helpful to know. Asylum seekers – the ones who receive 'taxpayers' money and benefits in kind' are, of course, not allowed to work. I can't imagine the writer is saying asylum seekers should be told they will get nothing if they flee here. 'Immigrants' are so often accused of coming here and taking jobs because they are prepared to work for less, it is hard to see how telling them they would receive nothing from the state would deter them.

Info

Jewish Voices

The European Jewish Press asked British Jews' views on how they feel about being Jewish today in the United Kingdom:

Marcia Goodman, 63, social work manager, originally from Manchester but now living in London, said: "Being Jewish is a very important aspect of my life although I am not religiously observant.

"As far as the future is concerned I feel that with the resurgence of modern orthodoxy amongst many young families the community in Britain will continue with similar numbers and similar influence as at present.

"I do not perceive a bias towards Jews in the media but there is certainly a bias against Israel which is to great extent based on ignorance of the historical facts.

"I am fortunate in that I have not personally experienced anti-Semitism but I am aware that many Jews in this country have been the subject of physical and verbal abuse.

"Obviously the ever growing numbers of Muslim immigrants into this country will constitute a threat to the security of the Jewish community."

Andrew Berg, 30, foreign exchange trader, from London, said: "In a country where religion is visibly in decline, I think being a Jew in Britain is more challenging than it has ever been. Finding a balance between religious observance and tradition seems to be a struggle for most people and it is no different for me.

"Recently I decided to explore our religion a bit deeper. I wanted to know more having forgotten much from my childhood. I was surprised to see how welcomed I was."

Hilary Tammer, 58, an assistant tax consultant from Leeds, said: "Being Jewish is an integral part of who I am and how I conduct my life. I am extremely proud to be Jewish and as a British Jew regard myself as fortunate to have the freedom to practice my religion freely.

"I am aware that the statistics point to a shrinking of Jewish communities for many reasons, but I am still convinced that British Jewry will continue to thrive.

"I have observed a lot of unjustified bias against Jews and Israel in the media leading to much frustration on my part. This is particularly prevalent on certain TV discussion programmes. However from time to time I have been uplifted to see and read unsolicited praise expressed towards matters Jewish and Israeli.

"On one or two occasions I have personally encountered antipathy directed towards Jews generally and Israel in particular. On these rare occasions I have always spoken up and made my feelings clear.

"Being tolerant is of course a two way street. We should all endeavour to learn something about other religions as ignorance leads to misunderstanding and misunderstanding leads to fear.

"Personally I am always happy to explain about our religious festivals and similarly I am keen to learn about the festivals of other faiths."

Jewish cemetery in East Ham

19 "Europe's Tarnished Golden Door?"

The EU enlargement of 2004 and the influx of new immigrants which followed it provoked a fresh debate on the effects of immigration within the UK, particularly in the light of increased pressure on the borders of the EU from people desperate to escape poverty and oppression in other parts of the world. In this extract from a BBC radio documentary, the presenter Quentin Peel gathers views from experts Sir Digby Jones, representing industry, John Monks, a trade-unionist, Sir Andrew Green, a critic of immigration, Sarah Spencer and Danny Sriskandarajah, who are academics, about the effects of immigration and the prospects for the future. – BBC Radio 4: *Analysis: Europe's Tarnished Golden Door?*, broadcast 30 March & 2 April 2006.

PEEL: Just look around you. Migrants from the east are changing the face of immigration in Britain and western Europe. Workers from the ten new member states of the European Union are taking advantage of free labour movement. Strange Slavonic tongues can be heard from the construction sites of Camberwell to the mushroom farms of Monaghan. But who's benefiting? Sir Digby Jones is director general of the Confederation of British Industry.

JONES: Oh, it's excellent for business! We haven't got enough skilled people. We've made the leap to a restructured economic society far more quickly and certainly more recently than France or Germany, and we actually need more and better skilled people, and, frankly, we ain't growing enough of our own.

GREEN: He would say that, wouldn't he? Employers are laughing all the way to the bank. What they can do is to get skilled workers off the shelf – no training costs, un-unionized and quite possibly at a lower level of pay. It's lovely!

PEEL: Sir Andrew Green, chairman of Migration-Watch UK.

GREEN: In a welfare state, there is no such thing as cheap labour. It's simply that the other costs, the costs of infrastructure and so on, are met by the taxpayer. So if you're an employer, you're very happy; if you're a worker, you've got reason for concern.

PEEL: Job-seekers from central and eastern Europe are the latest contributors to an upsurge in net migration into Britain over the past decade. They're young, bright and hard-working, and they're taking jobs everywhere from cafes to care work. [...] Sir Andrew Green's think-tank, MigrationWatch UK, is worried about Britain's capacity to take in so many people.

GREEN: Our problem with the present scale of immigration is that it is having a major impact on our infrastructure and on our community relations. Foreign immigration is running now at a third of a million every year. We simply don't think that's sensible, we don't think we can absorb that number of people. [...] British emigration is of the order of one hundred and twenty thousand a year. I see no reason why we should not have inward migration of a similar level. That should be quite enough.

PEEL: That sounds neat and tidy. But is it? Sarah Spencer is associate director of the Centre on Migration Policy and Society at Oxford University, and a member of the Commission for Racial Equality.

SPENCER: There has been an increase. It's not very meaningful as a total figure because we're talking about such very different people. There are people who are coming for family reunion; there are people coming for asylum who may or may not stay in the long-term; there are students who come for a short or longer period to study – and indeed to work; and then there are labour migrants. [...] I think it is important to recognize that migration isn't something that you can turn on and off like a tap – and also governments are anxious to reassure the public that immigration is under control. In fact, it is enormously difficult to control because we're talking about complex pull factors – not least the fact that employers very much want people to come and work here – and also a range of push factors, not least for people fleeing and wanting to claim asylum. The danger of trying to close a gate – for instance, saying we won't have any more low-skilled workers – is that if the demand is still there for them, then those jobs are going to be filled; and if they're not filled by legal workers coming in through a legal channel then somebody else is going to take those jobs.

PEEL: In other words, on the black market. It's not just the huddled masses that are knocking at the door. The number of asylum seekers has dropped significantly, but now our own economic growth is pulling would-be workers in. [...] Does John Monks, the British general secretary of the European Trade Union Confederation, see a threat to his members from these new eastern invaders?

MONKS: Free movement of labour – and now it's the twenty-five countries, plus one or two others actually – is what the EU is all about, and we recognize that if you're in favour of the European Union, you've got to be in favour of that as well. Its value, though, is, I think, proven, although there are many difficulties. The fact is that with an ageing population in many of Western European countries, it's important that migration is encouraged. It's done a lot for the British economy and it'll do a lot for a lot of other economies as well.

PEEL: Can you be a bit more specific about how economic migration would actually benefit, for example, workers in Britain then?

MONKS: Well, at the moment, the migrants tend to be doing jobs that it's quite hard to find the British ready to do. Although we've got alarming pockets of high unemployment, there's still major problems in finding people who'll go picking in the fields and serving in the cafés and working unsocial hours in hotels. And these migrant workers have done those jobs. They've been doing it since the war. West Indians and others came in. Now the main thrust has switched to central and eastern Europe. But I'm astonished and delighted by the absence of tensions. Of course, if it was ten per cent unemployment – as it is in Germany – it would be rather different. [...]

PEEL: In 1999, for the first time, the largest group of immigrants came from non-Commonwealth and non-EU countries. What does Danny Sriskandarajah, head of migration studies at the Institute for Public Policy Research in London, think are the implications?

SRISKANDARAJAH: Britain's multiculturalist policies have been about broad categories, defining people, almost a tick-a-box approach to multiculturalism – you're black, you're white, you're Asian. The reality is much, much more complex; that even within a group such as black Africans, we're seeing incredible diversity, for example, in socio-economic outcomes. Nigerians and Somalis will both tick the black African box. But in socio-economic terms they are at different ends of the profile – they have incredibly different rates of employment, incredibly different average incomes – and so unless we come to terms with that diversity policy interventions just won't be effective. On the ground, I think we also need to think about how public service delivery comes to terms with something like super-diversity. For far too long our public service provision, when it comes to education or healthcare, has been about targeting the needs of a particular minority. That might work if you have fifteen per cent of a population which consists of one ethnic minority. It might not work when there are fifteen different groups, each making up one per cent of the community. It's that challenge of tackling super-diversity that we need to be aware of.

PEEL: Britain's more super-diverse in its immigrant population than the rest of Europe; partly because the English language is such a magnet. [...] Our prosperous European continent acts as a fatal attraction, especially to its near abroad. Well managed, immigration can be of great mutual benefit: providing skills to the developed economies when they need them, remittances for migrant workers to send to their families and training – as well as seed capital – for those who want to return home.

Trying to close the golden door will only create a miserable buffer zone, where impoverished migrants clamour for admittance. We shouldn't close the door, even if we could. Instead, we should export our prosperity and seek to close the income gap. We should encourage more two-way movement. It may not ease Europe's economic pull, but it would alleviate the push of the huddled masses.

Vocabulary

Title: to tarnish (v.): become less bright and attractive - **17 to benefit** (v.): to gain or give an advantage - **23 to restructure** (v.): to change the economy (i.e. to more modern industries) - **26 frankly ... ain't:** used as a humorous catch-phrase with a dialect short form of 'are not' - **29 off the shelf:** immediately available - **30 un-unionized** (adj.): not part of a trade union - **36 infrastructure** (n.): the organizational systems of a country, e.g. providing housing, health care, education, pensions, etc. - **40 net** (adj.): overall amount (here: how many more come in than go out) - **48 community relations** (n.): relations between different sections of the population, particularly those different in race or origin - **63 family reunion** (n.): bringing dependents to join family members - **116 tick-a-box approach** (n.): way of dealing with something by making simple choices - **126 intervention** (n.): here: measures, taking action - **142 its near abroad** (n.): foreign countries not far away from it - **143 of great mutual benefit:** good for both sides - **145 remittance** (n.): money sent to s.o. - **146 seed capital** (n.): money to start a new business - **149 miserable** (adj.): sad, poor - **149 buffer zone** (n.): area outside a state, designed to protect it - **154 to alleviate** (v.): to make s.th. less bad

Explanations

14 Camberwell: part of South London - **16 Monaghan:** a county in the northern part of Eire - **19f. Confederation of British Industry:** organization of employers, representing companies - **27 He would say that, wouldn't he?:** well-known humorous catch-phrase to dismiss someone's statement, made famous by Mandy Rice-Davies in a 1963 trial when a lord denied having an affair with her - **32f. MigrationWatch UK:** an 'independent and non-political' organization which opposes immigration - **59 Commission for Racial Equality:** an organization set up by law in 1976 to improve relations between races and prevent discrimination - **111f. Institute for Public Policy Research:** an organization set up to discuss social issues, which investigated immigration from a positive point of view

Awareness

1 Should people be able to live and work where they want? If not, why not?

Comprehension

2 What differences in immigration to the UK have been seen in recent years?
3 What is meant by 'push' and 'pull' factors?
4 Why does the text suggest that a particularly large quantity of immigrants want to come to the UK?
5 What is Peel's conclusion about how Europe should act in future?

Analysis

6 Use the views expressed in the programme to list the advantages and disadvantages of immigration.
7 Explain the allusion to the 'huddled masses' (ll. 84 and 155).
8 How does Danny Sriskandarajah think priorities in dealing with immigrants will have to change?
9 Show how the presenter uses provocative questions or opinions as cues for his interviewees.
10 Analyse the language used by the presenter and his interviewees. For instance, look particularly at the register (formal or informal), rhetorical devices, idiomatic phrases and ways of expressing number, amount or degree.

Opinion

11 Organize a debate about immigration.
12 In an age of globalization, what is the effect of restricting the movement of people?

Projects

13 Find out more about migration within the EU, and immigration to the EU, and what different EU countries are doing about it. What happens to people who apply to enter, or try to enter illegally?

20

John Agard

"Encounter"

John Agard was born in Guyana in 1949. His father was Portuguese and his mother Guyanese. Since he came to Britain in 1977 he has written numerous collections of poetry for adults and children, as well as plays and stories. He regularly performs his poetry at festivals and in schools. David Dabydeen has written: "John Agard's poetry is a wonderful affirmation of life, in a language that is as vital and joyous as we are able to craft it in the Caribbean, in spite of our history of distress." John Agard lives in Sussex with the poet Grace Nichols and their family. – John Agard, 'Encounter' in *We Brits* (Tarset: Bloodaxe, 2006), p. 68.

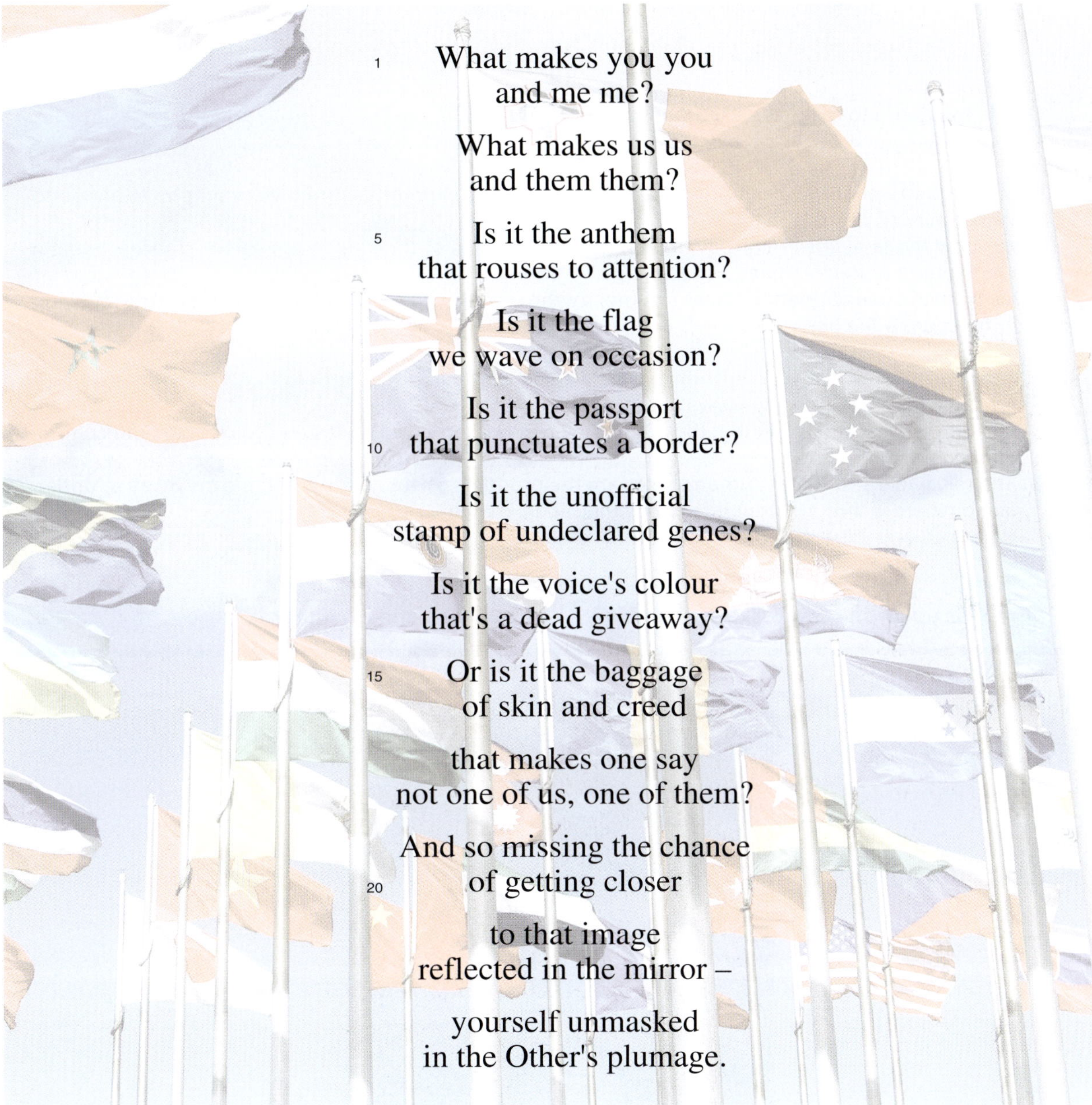

What makes you you
and me me?

What makes us us
and them them?

Is it the anthem
that rouses to attention?

Is it the flag
we wave on occasion?

Is it the passport
that punctuates a border?

Is it the unofficial
stamp of undeclared genes?

Is it the voice's colour
that's a dead giveaway?

Or is it the baggage
of skin and creed

that makes one say
not one of us, one of them?

And so missing the chance
of getting closer

to that image
reflected in the mirror –

yourself unmasked
in the Other's plumage.

Vocabulary

6 attention (n.): interest and notice; standing straight with arms by your sides and feet together – **8 on occasion** (n.): from time to time; for a special event or celebration – **10 to punctuate** (v.): to divide a sentence with special marks; to make a hole in s.th. – **12 undeclared** (adj.): not spoken aloud to others; not officially announced to customs officers – **14 dead giveaway** (n.): (infml) s.th. that makes it really easy to see what is supposed to be hidden – **15 baggage** (n.): bags etc. you carry when travelling; opinions, beliefs etc. which cause problems that are not really necessary – **24 plumage** (n.): covering of feathers, often distinctive and brightly-coloured

Explanation

Intro/3 David Dabydeen: a leading Caribbean-British novelist, poet and broadcaster

Awareness

1 List the groups you think you belong to (nationality, gender, class, race, hair colour, fashion preferences etc.).

Comprehension

2 Divide the poem to make the argument clear.

Analysis

3 Go through the poem analysing the imagery and semantic potential in its stanzas (pay attention to the ambiguity of words)

4 Show how the final lines might overcome the binary ways of thinking in the earlier stanzas. Explain the metaphors of mirror, mask and plumage.

5 Investigate the use of poetic devices (rhyme, rhythm, assonance, alliteration, repetition etc.) showing their function in the poem.

Opinion

6 There are two main opposing views about culture and identity:

a) The universalists maintain that there are universal human experiences and values beneath cultural differences.

b) The relativists assert that human values are the products of our cultures and the only way to understand others is through understanding cultural difference.

Where do you think the poem stands on this issue?

Project

7 Using the poem and other texts in this book, how could we define identity?

The poets Grace Nichols and John Agard, born in Guyana, now live in Sussex

Competence Training

You can use this Viewfinder to practise most or all of the skills you will need to satisfy the requirements set out in the European Frame of Reference (up to level C1) and tested in exams like the German *Abitur* (all *Bundesländer*), TOEFL and IELTS, or the International Baccalaureate.

Details about all the skills (often referred to in German as *Kompetenzen*) that you can work to improve, and which of the texts and/or sections from the book will be most useful in doing it are set out on these pages. They provide cross-references to the Viewfinder Reference Library (RL), where you can find out exactly how to do things. You will get the RL from your teacher or you can download it from http://www.langenscheidt.de. At the end there is a revision checklist to make sure you can remember the main points the book deals with. This can be used for exam revision.

Language skills

Basic and advanced language skills
- grammar/structure
- vocabulary (new words, word formation)
- idiom
- register

Oral skills
- pronunciation
- intonation
- presentation

Written skills
- spelling
- punctuation
- text layout

All the texts in this book can help you practise and extend your competence in the active language skills of **speaking** and **writing** and the receptive skills of **reading** and **listening**. You should have learnt the basic language skills in English before you started working with this book. If you're not very confident yet, don't worry. You'll be able to practise all these skills and bring them up to a more advanced level working with any of the texts here. Some of the tasks are better for oral skills and others for written skills. Try to learn new words in their contexts (without trying to find the equivalent in your own language), and note down points which give you trouble, concentrating on learning them and checking your work specially to make sure you don't make the same mistake again. You will find a lot of helpful material in the RL.

Speaking
- ability to pronounce English correctly (using correct accent and intonation)
- ability to use different idioms and registers
- managing discourse (making an appropriate choice of vocabulary, sentence structure, rhetorical devices, text structure) in, for example, everyday conversation or presentations

Reading
- comprehension of content
- understanding a writer's train of thought
- ability to recognise and understand a variety of text types, fictional and non-fictional

Listening
- comprehension of content
- ability to understand a variety of spoken text types (conversations, news broadcasts, talks, speeches)
- being aware of rhetorical devices used by speakers
- ability to understand different social and geographical accents and dialects

Writing
- ability to spell and punctuate correctly
- ability to write a number of different text types (essay, letter, report, presentation, commentary, analysis) using the appropriate vocabulary, grammar, register and text structure

Don't forget: mistakes can be useful because you can learn from them, but repeated mistakes are a waste of time. The more proficient your English is, the more fun it will be to use, and the better impression it will make on your communication partners.

Text types

This volume contains examples of the following types of texts which you will be asked to analyse:

non-fictional texts	
newspaper report	texts 1 (extra), 6, 7, 8, 16
newspaper comment article	text 18
internet discussion thread	text 18
radio programme (transcript)	text 19
speech	texts 1, 3
fictional texts	
novel	texts 2, 4, 10, 11, 12, 14, 15, 17
short story	text 13
screenplay	text 9
comedy sketch	text 8 (pp. 32f.)
dub poem	text 5
poem	text 20
visual texts	
photographs	particularly texts 1, 4, 16, 17
cartoons	texts 3, 7

Particular study skills when approaching texts

The tasks and questions which follow each text are designed to develop skills in a number of areas: language practice and understanding, analysing and appreciating a wide variety of fictional and non-fictional texts. The tasks will also enable you to develop your own ideas on the topics dealt with, and motivate you to carry out further research into areas that interest you.

AWARENESS:
Before reading a text you should be aware of certain ideas, facts, expectations or prejudices which form the context of the text itself. A skill to practise in all texts is:
note-taking; this is a key skill for
a) preparing for discussions and
b) reading and analysing texts (see below)

Other skills to practise here include:

COLLECTING AND COLLATING IDEAS:

brainstorming (RL B 2)	texts 3 (question 1), 5(1), 10(1), 12(1), 13(1), 16(1), 17(1)
mind map (RL A 5)	texts 10(1), 13(2), 16(1), 20(1)
list	text 20(1)
flow chart (RL A 5)	text 11(2)
question and answer session	texts 8(1), 13(2)
reports on individual experience	texts 1(1), 6(1), 9(1)
general discussion	texts 12(2), 19(1)
library research	texts 11(1), 15(1), 18(2)
internet research (RL A 6)	texts 2(1), 7(2), 9(2), 11(2), 13(1), 14(1), 15(1), 18(1,2)
practical research	texts 4(1), 6(1), 8(2)
role-play	text 7(1)

DURING READING YOU CAN PRACTISE A NUMBER OF SKILLS:
– skimming for general impressions
– scanning to find out facts or information
– note-making (RL A 4)

– marking important passages
– deducing meanings from context
– using a monolingual dictionary (RL A 3)
– using a bilingual dictionary (RL A 3)
– dividing the text
– summarising (RL C 3)
– finding the deeper meaning
– appreciating aesthetic qualities

In this *Viewfinder* volume you can practise all these skills on any text. Usually, apart from skimming, you will need to read a text at least three times. The questions under the heading 'Comprehension' are designed for the first seven skills on the list; the 'Analysis' questions will help you practise the last three skills.

AFTER READING:
After you have read the text there are 'Analysis' and 'Opinion' questions to help you discover more meaning in the text, and think about what it means for you personally or what its implications are. You can do these questions alone, in pairs or groups, or as a class. You can answer them individually, present your answers to a plenum, or present them in writing.

Individual written answers can be in the form of clearly organised notes or an essay.
Individual oral answers can be, e.g., in the form of a presentation based on notes.
Make sure your answers are clear and concise and relevant.
Check that your listeners have understood your answer.

Answers can also be produced orally or in writing in pair-work or group-work. This will enable you to practise the following teamwork skills:
– using the opportunity of practising English without being supervised
– organizing and dividing up tasks
– co-operating and pooling ideas and skills
– using appropriate research tools
– practising time-management skills (keeping to a timetable)
– choosing an appropriate type of presentation
– using media as presentation aids.

The 'Opinion' questions can be used for various forms of discussion, argument or debate.
These can be used to practise oral communication skills (see RL B 2). The following tasks are particularly suitable:
texts 3(10), 5(7), 7(10), 8(10), 10(7), 14(11), 15(11), 16(14), 17(12), 19(11)

Textual analysis skills

The text analysis questions form the core of your coursework in English in the *Oberstufe* and their aim is to help you
a) work out what meanings the text might have for you and other readers
b) discover how the text affects you and the means used to achieve this
c) make judgments and write about the content of the text, its value, and its relevance to you.

NON-FICTIONAL TEXTS:

establishing types of text (RL C 1.2.1)	e.g. newspaper report: texts 1 (extra text), 6, 7, 16; newspaper feature: text 8; newspaper comment article: text 18; speech: texts 1, 3; radio programme transcript: text 19; internet discussion thread: text 18; spoof analysis: text 8 (Goodness Gracious Who?)
content (fact v. opinion etc) (RL C 1.2.1)	texts 1(9,15), 3(5,7), 7(7), 16(6–12), 18(7), 19 (9,10)

structure and form (RL C 1.2.1)	texts 1(7,12), 3(4), 6(3–5), 7(5–6), 16(5), 18(6)
function (RL C 1.2.2)	texts 1(9), 3(8), 6(6), 7(7), 8(8,9), 16(7,11,12), 19(5)
style and tone (RL C 1.2.2)	texts 1(10,11), 3(5–7), 8(5,9), 16(6,9), 18(8), 19(9,10)
recognizing humour and irony	texts 8(7,9,12), 18(10), 19(10)
integrating visual components	text 16
FICTIONAL TEXTS:	
genre (RL C 1.1)	texts 2(8,9), 4(14), 5(1,8), 8(two sketches: 6), 9(11), 11, 15(9), 20(2–5)
theme (RL C 1.1)	texts 2(7,10), 4(12,14), 5(5), 9(9), 11(10,12), 12(4), 13(9,11), 17(10), 20(6,7)
character and characterisation (RL C 1.1)	texts 2(6,9), 4(6,7,11), 8(9) 9(6,7), 10(4), 11(6), 12(5,6,9), 13(8,12), 14(5,6), 15(7), 17(7,8)
setting and atmosphere (RL C 1.1)	texts 4(8), 11(4,11), 13(10), 15(5), 17(6)
structure and formal aspects (RL C 1.1)	texts 5(5), 8(two sketches: 5,6), 20(2)
style (RL C 1.1)	texts 2(6b), 4(7,8,10), 10(3), 11(6,10), 13(6,7), 14(4,9), 15(9), 20(3,4,5)
tone (RL C 1.1)	texts 2(6), 4(11,14), 5(6), 8(9), 10(3), 11(6), 12(9), 13(6,7,12), 15(6,9), 17(7)

Listening comprehension skills

Any of the texts can be used for listening comprehension if you listen to someone reading them, make notes and answer questions or summarize the text. Texts that are particularly useful are those where

the author can be heard:	texts 5(2), 10
texts and music	texts 5(1,8), 17(13)

Visual text comprehension skills

reading cartoons	texts 3(11), 7
analysing films (RL C 2.2)	texts 8, 9
comparing text and film	texts 7(12), 13(14,15), 14(13)

Particular writing skills / creative writing skills

that you can practise in 'Projects' or on the whole text:

essay	any text
paper	any text
report	texts 1(16,17), 2(10,11,12), 4(15,17), 6(7), 7(11), 8(11,12), 9(10,12), 10(8), 11(14), 12(10,11,12), 13(13) 14(14,15),15(10-13), 17(14), 18(13,14), 19(13), 20(7)
book report	texts 4(18), 10(10), 11(15), 13(15)
letter	texts 3(9), 16(15)
e-mail	text 7(8)
poem / song	text 5(8)
interior monologue	text 14(10)
dialogue / conversation	text 4(16)
sketch	text 8 (two sketches: 6)
blog	text 17(15)
internet discussion thread	text 18(11)

Intercultural Skills

Intercultural linguistic skills:
When you use another language you need intercultural skills. This is because languages do not just have different words; they differ fundamentally in the ways they express thoughts, or even sometimes in the thoughts they choose to express. So there is no such thing as word-for-word or exact translation. Just think, e.g., of the differences between the German word *fahren* and the English *drive*. Or where, in German, you might write: "Mit diesem Bild will der Autor die Unmenschlichkeit des Krieges ausdrücken", in English we might say "The author uses this image to express the horrors of war."

So when working with this book you need to develop skills in relation to the use of the foreign language:

- **Intercultural linguistic awareness:** e.g. seeing how differently words and structures are used in English from their 'equivalents' in your language;
- **Intercultural linguistic competence:** e.g. being able to use the foreign language in the way that members of that language community use and understand it;
- **Register and tone:** e.g. being able to recognize and use different registers like academic or colloquial, or different tones like serious, humorous or sarcastic.

All the texts and tasks in this volume expect you to work in the medium of English, which will help you to practise these vital skills.

Specifically, you may be required to actively use various types of equivalents between English and your own language. This will involve the following skills:

- **Translation** (German: *Übersetzung*): Here you must try to find the nearest possible written equivalent in the other language while making sure that it reads like an original text in terms of structure, idiom, register and tone. This is particularly difficult in literary texts where you have to think of the aesthetic effect as well.
- **Interpreting** (German: *dolmetschen*): As an interpreter you must try to give the nearest equivalent possible of someone's spoken words, either after they have said them, or simultaneously.
- **Conveying the sense** (German: *Mediation*): People may want to know the sense, or message, of a document. They need to know the important facts and figures, but the particular linguistic expressions used in the original are irrelevant.

The texts in this *Viewfinder* volume (or extracts from them) most suitable for translating or conveying the sense are: texts 1, 3, 6, 7, 16, 18, 19. You could also convey the sense of particular positions, like those of the characters in texts 12, 13 and 14. For a real challenge you could try to translate the poem in text 20.

In addition, this Viewfinder volume *Ethnic Diversity in the UK* also deals specifically with the interactions of different cultures, and so is particularly useful for practising other intercultural skills:

intercultural awareness and familiarization	introductory text, texts 2, 4, 5, 8, 9, 10, 11, 12, 13, 14, 15, 17, 18, 20
empathising with others	introductory text, texts 1 (extra text); 2, 4, 7, 9, 10, 11, 12, 13, 14, 15, 17, 20
socio-historical contexts	texts 1, 2, 3, 4, 5, 6, 7, 8, 13, 17, 18, 19
contemporary problems	texts 1, 6, 7, 13, 14, 15, 16, 17, 18, 19

Particular tasks will give help in practising these skills:

ethnicity and identity	texts 1(1,14,17), 2(1,10,11,12), 4(13), 6(6), 7(1), 9(2,10,11), 10(5,8), 12(2,4), 13(5,10), 17(14) 18(2,12), 19(8), 20(1,6,7)
language and dialect	texts 2(5), 4(10), 5(3), 9(7), 10(3),11(5,6,7), 17(8,9)
religion	texts 5(1) (Rastafari), 9(2,6,8) (Sikhism), 13(2,13), 14(1,3,10,12,15), 15(2,3) (Islam and comparison of religions), 18(12,13) (Judaism)
cultural assumptions and particularities	texts 1(1,6,7,14), 2(7), 3(6), 4(9,15), 8(7, sketches 2), 9(3,5,6,9), 10(5), 11(5,12), 12(1,2,12), 13(2,4,10), 14(3,8,9,10,13,14), 15(2,6,9), 18(2,3,12,13), 20(1,4)
prejudices and stereotypes	texts 2(7,8). 3(1,3,5), 4(13,16), 7(1), 8(7,9), 10(6), 13(7,12), 15(6,8), 16(6,7,8,11,12), 18(3,7,9),
integration and equality	texts 1(7,8,11,12,13), 3(3,4), 4(13,14), 6(2,3,6), 7(6,9,10,11,12), 8(8), 12(4,12), 18(14), 19(8)
conflicts and reactions	1(16), 3(8), 4(12), 5(5,6,7), 6(2,4,5,6), 9(1), 10(2), 12(1,9), 13(11), 14(11,14), 18(12)
relativism and universality	11(12), 12(1), 14(12), 15(3),17(10), 20(6,7)

Revision

As preparation for exams and assessments, it is a good idea to revise the main points you have learnt in this Viewfinder volume. The information may be useful if you are asked questions about this topic, or as background knowledge to put other things into context. In any event, if you are sure about these points it will boost your confidence.

Key terms and concepts

ethnic diversity	from ethnic minorities to super-diversity	Who is there in the UK?
identity	according to ethnic origins hyphenated identity 2nd generation	Who are they?
	'Britishness'	Who are we? (social cohesion)
	citizenship (definitions of 'Britishness'?) choosing identity	legal status (imagined community) (imagined identity)
immigrant migrant member of ethnic group	(compare: 'foreigner')	'push' and 'pull' factors
refugee/asylum-seeker economic migrant illegal immigrant	(compare: 'failed asylum-seeker') (compare: 'bogus asylum-seeker')	
integration	'two-way street' Trevor Phillips: equality, participation, interaction	ways of living together influencing one another
assimilation segregation		adopting 'host' identity leading separate lives
xenophobia racism		hatred of foreigners
discrimination	to discriminate against s.o. direct indirect	in housing, employment, leisure
prejudice stereotype		unjustified ideas
legislation positive action	anti-discrimination legislation (v. affirmative action, positive discrimination)	for equality of opportunity
political correctness	(PC)	changing attitudes

Make-up of ethnic diversity

Although there was ethnic diversity in the UK before 1945, we distinguish particular groups post-1945. Those referred to in this volume are:

White English		text 7
Caribbean	'Windrush generation' (Afro- and Indo-Caribbean)	texts 2, 3, 4, 5, 6, 10, 1, 20
Indian	(Hindu, Sikh)	texts 3, 9, 10, 8
Pakistani		texts 3, 13, 14
Bangladeshi		texts 11, 12
Chinese		text 11
East African	(Muslim)	text 15
Polish		texts 17, 19
Portuguese/Brazilian		texts 17, 19
Jewish		text 18
Romany		text 17

'Milestones'

Empire Windrush arrival	1948	'Great Insurrection'	1981-3
Notting Hill riots	1958	Stephen Lawrence case	1993-9
Enoch Powell speech	1968	EU enlargement	2004
National Front marches	1970s	London bombings (7/7)	2005

Problems associated with ethnic diversity

race and colour	prejudice, stereotypes, racism, discrimination	largely historical

contemporary problems:

identity and super-diversity	questions of 'Britishness'
immigration	opposition to further immigration
preserving cultural identity	v. integration
asylum	resentment over 'bogus' asylum-seekers
2nd generation	immigrants and their children
Islamist extremism	
'PC gone mad'	state intervention v. self-sufficiency
role of press and media	

Elements of integration / appreciating diversity

legislation and institutions
writing
music and dance
films

humour
cuisine
dress

Differences from German situation

prejudice and stereotyping	still more prevalent in Germany than in the UK
historical ties	more UK immigration is related to the colonial past
language	most UK immigrants have English as first or second language, so have fewer problems
EU immigration	Germany restricted Eastern European immigration

Contents of Reference Library